DATE DUE

AP 23 98			
MY 14 98			
DE 19 08			

DEMCO 38-296

The Power of Separation

PRINCETON STUDIES IN AMERICAN POLITICS:
HISTORICAL, INTERNATIONAL, AND COMPARATIVE PERSPECTIVES

SERIES EDITORS

IRA KATZNELSON, MARTIN SHEFTER, THEDA SKOCPOL

Labor Visions and State Power: The Origins of Business Unionism in the United States by Victoria C. Hattam

The Lincoln Persuasion: Remaking American Liberalism by J. David Greenstone

Politics and Industrialization: Early Railroads in the United States and Prussia by Colleen A. Dunlavy

Political Parties and the State: The American Historical Experience by Martin Shefter

Prisoners of Myth: The Leadership of the Tennessee Valley Authority, 1933–1990 by Erwin C. Hargrove

Bound by Our Constitution: Women, Workers, and the Minimum Wage by Vivien Hart

Experts and Politicians: Reform Challenges to Machine Politics in New York, Cleveland, and Chicago by Kenneth Finegold

Social Policy in the United States: Future Possibilities in Historical Perspective by Theda Skocpol

Political Organizations by James Q. Wilson

Facing Up to the American Dream: Race, Class, and the Soul of the Nation by Jennifer L. Hochschild

Classifying by Race edited by Paul E. Peterson

From the Outside In: World War II and the American State by Bartholomew H. Sparrow

Kindred Strangers: The Uneasy Relationship between Politics and Business in America by David Vogel

Why Movements Succeed or Fail: Opportunity, Culture, and the Struggle for Woman Suffrage by Lee Ann Banaszak

The Power of Separation: American Constitutionalism and the Myth of the Legislative Veto by Jessica Korn

The
Power of
Separation

AMERICAN CONSTITUTIONALISM
AND THE MYTH OF THE
LEGISLATIVE VETO

Jessica Korn

Princeton University Press
Princeton, New Jersey

Copyright © 1996 by Princeton University Press
Published by Princeton University Press, 41 William Street,
Princeton, New Jersey 08540
In the United Kingdom: Princeton University Press, Chichester, West Sussex

Library of Congress Cataloging-in-Publication Data

Korn, Jessica, 1966–
    The power of separation : American constitutionalism and the myth
of the legislative veto / Jessica Korn.
        p.   cm. — (Princeton studies in American politics)
    Includes bibliographical references and index.
    ISBN 0-691-02135-X (cl : alk. paper)
    1. Separation of powers—United States.   2. Legislative veto—
United States.   I. Title.   II. Series.
JK305.K67   1996
320.473—dc20   96-2193
                                                        CIP

This book has been composed in Times Roman

Princeton University Press books are printed on acid-free paper and meet the guidelines
for permanence and durability of the Committee on Production Guidelines for Book
Longevity of the Council on Library Resources

Printed in the United States of America by Princeton Academic Press

1 3 5 7 9 10 8 6 4 2

DEDICATED TO MY PARENTS,
ADOLFO AND SUSANA KORN

CONTENTS

The Power of Separation

Chapter One

INTRODUCTION:
AMERICAN CONSTITUTIONALISM AND
AMERICAN POLITICAL SCIENCE

As a new wave of democratization sweeps the world, political scientists and reformers have turned with keen interest to the study of the American political system, the oldest on-going experiment in constitutional democracy. Partly inspired by constitution writers in Eastern Europe, Latin America, and Africa who have felt compelled to consider the history of American constitutionalism, political scientists are asking old questions with a new urgency about the actual functioning of American political institutions. Foremost among these questions is whether the American constitutional order, designed in the eighteenth century for a fledgling, agrarian nation, can fulfill the governing needs of an industrial superpower in the twentieth century. Today, answers to this question inform whether and how the lessons of American constitutional politics can serve as a guide to emerging democracies, and also whether American political institutions themselves are in need of reform.[1]

Since Woodrow Wilson became the first political scientist to pronounce the American constitutional structure obsolete for the governing demands of the twentieth century, the dominant assumption underlying studies of American political institutions has been that the

Constitution suffers from fundamental structural defects. Wilson directed his attack against the doctrine of the separation of powers embodied in the Constitution. He believed it antithetical to the expansion and centralization of federal power made necessary by the profound political and social changes caused, at the turn of the century, by large-scale urbanization, immigration, and industrialization.[2]

Early in his career as a political scientist, Wilson called for reforms that would make the constitutional structure more like a parliamentary system. Once executive powers were subsumed within the legislative branch, Wilson argued, Congress would become capable of properly authorizing and guiding the administration of new governmental programs. He also believed such reforms would endow Congress with the leadership powers necessary to bring a wide variety of interests behind one comprehensive policy vision.[3]

Wilson later changed his mind about how best to reform American government, calling upon presidents to subordinate legislative power to executive branch leadership and claiming that such constitutional reform could be achieved without actual constitutional amendment.[4] But his political science was consistent in its diagnosis that the existing separation of powers system, left to its own purposes, would inevitably thwart the necessary evolution of governmental powers. Interestingly, while Wilson's practical political experience as president led him to question some of the claims of his own scholarly writings, his critique of constitutional structure became, and remains, "axiomatic" and "commonplace" for many students of American politics.[5]

The legislative veto was one of the most highly touted of the many proposals to reform constitutional structure that emerged out of the Wilsonian critique of the Constitution. Once it was actually enacted into law, it captivated the attention of those intent on counteracting the alleged flaws of the separation of powers system.[6] The legislative veto was supposed to enhance administrative leadership in the system by making it easier for members of Congress to delegate new powers to the executive. By attaching legislative veto provisions to delegated powers, members guaranteed themselves prior review of the proposed uses of these powers, together with a way to disallow, or "veto," any such proposed uses without having to pass a new law.

The new legislative veto procedure enabled members to reduce the formal separation between legislative and administrative responsibilities by authorizing Congress to bypass the constitutional bicameralism and presentment clauses. These clauses require any formal legislative action to be approved by both chambers of Congress and presented to the president. With the legislative veto, members could shortcut these requirements in a variety of ways, depending on the particular form of the mechanism they had attached to the delegation of authority in question: a two-house veto authorized them to reject a proposed action by passing a resolution through both chambers, a one-house veto required a resolution through either chamber, and a committee veto demanded simply approval or disapproval by specified committees.

First enacted into law in the Reorganization Act of 1932, the legislative veto originated as a bargaining chip with which to allow the president to enhance his management capacities. President Herbert Hoover never implemented the broad reorganization powers delegated to him in 1932.[7] But members renewed this delegation, again subject to legislative veto review, in the Reorganization Act of 1939, and chose not to veto President Franklin Roosevelt's proposed use of this new authority. Consequently, Roosevelt succeeded in implementing what remains today the most comprehensive restructuring of executive power ever imposed by an American president.[8]

But the veto mechanism did not attract widespread attention until it began to serve a growing congressional demand for procedural weapons to restrain executive power.[9] Beginning in the late 1960s, as administrative agencies received broad new powers to engage in social and economic regulation, and especially as the Republican Nixon administration defied the policy objectives enacted by a Democratic-controlled Congress in the early 1970s, the number of legislative veto provisions enacted in statutes rose exponentially. Indeed, the legislative veto became representative of the "congressional resurgence" of the 1970s.[10] As a legal shortcut through the constitutionally mandated procedures for legislative action, it symbolized the lengths to which members were willing to go in order to fight back an "Imperial Presidency" and rein in the discretionary powers of bureaucrats.[11]

Some fifty years after its birth, the legislative veto landed on the front pages of newspapers around the country when the Supreme Court struck it down in *INS v Chadha* as a violation of the constitutional separation of powers.[12] The Supreme Court's decision, which came in 1983 during the first Reagan administration, seemed worthy of such attention because it promised a shift in the balance of policymaking power from Congress to the executive. A decade's worth of divided government—in which Republicans almost always controlled the White House and Democrats controlled Congress—had helped turn the legislative veto into a partisan lightning rod. As a mechanism thought to increase congressional control over policy outcomes, it was widely expected to hinder the implementation of Republican policies.

In the 1980s, partisans of the executive branch began to claim that the congressional resurgence of the 1970s had led to an "Imperial Congress" and a "Fettered Presidency."[13] They helped feed the fire of the legislative veto controversy by welcoming its invalidation as a victory for executive power. They urged the Supreme Court to continue fighting against "encroachments by the legislature."[14] In contrast, those who emphasized the need to protect congressional power from executive branch dominance viewed *Chadha* as a shortsighted, poorly reasoned decision based on a misunderstanding of the policymaking process.[15] Many saw it as confirmation that the Supreme Court was packed with partisan Republican judges intent on favoring a Republican White House.[16] Common to these opposing interpretations was the expectation that as long as the Republicans controlled the executive branch, *Chadha* portended increasingly Republican outcomes from the policymaking process.[17]

The Supreme Court's invalidation of the legislative veto also reached the front pages because it threatened to broaden the discretionary authorities of regulatory agencies. Since the legislative veto represented congressional restraint of administrative activities, observers worried that the mechanism's invalidation would leave regulatory agencies with too much unchecked power. Their worry sprang from the widely accepted critique of the American political system propounded by political scientists like Theodore Lowi. This critique describes the policymaking powers possessed by unelected bureaucrats—powers they obtain as a result of open-ended delegations of congressional authority—as sucking democratic accountability out of the federal government.[18] Consequently, the legislative veto appeared as "one of the most significant institutional developments in twentieth-century American politics" because it endowed Congress with extra-constitutional controls over delegated authorities.[19]

Justice White's dissent from the majority opinion in *Chadha* reinforced the view of the legislative veto as a policymaking instrument worthy of lavish attention. To White, it was senseless to strike down an "indispensable political invention that allows the President and Congress to resolve major constitutional and policy differences, assures the accountability of independent regulatory agencies, and preserves Congress's control over lawmaking."[20] His dissent has become a touchstone for the view in legal scholarship that preserving constitutional structure is antithetical to facilitating the necessary evolution of governmental processes.[21]

Justice White's argument for upholding the constitutionality of the legislative veto echoes the Wilsonian critique of the separation of powers as an obsolete and counterproductive governmental system for twentieth-century American politics. Indeed, although Wilson himself was not a student of the legislative veto issue, his critique of the separation of powers continues to provide the most explicit and comprehensive description of the analytical framework that has dominated legislative veto scholarship.

Observers in the 1970s and 1980s who viewed the legislative veto as "by far" Congress's "most powerful weapon" for reacting against the aggregation of foreign policymaking power in the presidency carried the Wilsonian conviction that the existing constitutional order was incompatible with powerful presidential leadership.[22] This conviction implied that Congress needed extra-constitutional mechanisms to combat the rise of extra-constitutional presidential powers. Consequently, it made the legislative veto seem uniquely valuable in the late twentieth century as analysts worried that the presidency had become too powerful.

Similarly, those who viewed the legislative veto as an indispensable counterpart to the creation of administrative agencies presumed that the separation of powers system was incapable of sustaining bureaucratic authority.[23] This Wilsonian belief meant that the actual establishment of administrative authority must have "substantially subverted the original constitutional understanding."[24] From this point of view, the legislative veto appeared essential because it established the extra-constitutional powers necessary to preserve Congress's rightful place in the policymaking process.

This book challenges the usefulness of the Wilsonian framework as a guide to understanding the political and constitutional significance of the legislative veto. In particular, I show that there was a striking disjunction between the minimal role actually played by the legislative veto and the great significance attributed to it by students of American politics. In exploring this disjunction, I call into question the unexamined belief built into Justice White's Wilsonian dissent: that American government cannot adapt to changing political circumstances unless it undergoes amendments to the procedures that separate executive and legislative power.

SIGNIFICANCE OF THE WILSONIAN FRAMEWORK

Examination of the exaggerated powers attributed to the legislative veto mechanism can be instructive to many contemporary students of American politics because Wilsonian convictions echo far beyond the legislative veto controversy. They reside in the core of the political science discipline, and reverberate through many analyses of the workings of American political institutions. In fact, the two prongs of the Wilsonian framework that made the legislative veto seem politically significant are the same two that have prevailed, in different forms throughout the twentieth century, as the focal points of inquiry for contemporary political scientists, legal scholars, and journalists observing American politics. One prong focuses on how the institutional separation of executive and legislative power in the Constitution thwarts the development of administrative capacities; the other focuses on how it hinders popular leadership.

With respect to administrative capacities, analysts have helped ensure the continuing vitality of the Wilsonian framework by blaming dysfunctional public policies on the arrangement of bureaucratic authority made necessary by constitutional structure. They note that at the turn of the century, to enable government to respond to growing demands for regulating the economy, Congress began delegating considerable lawmaking powers to independent regulatory agencies and to administrative agencies in the executive branch.[25] Other legislatures in industrialized countries faced similar demands at the time and produced similar solutions, thereby making the growth of administrative powers in the executive a worldwide phenomenon in the twentieth century. But in the face of this worldwide phenomenon, the constitutional separation of powers supposedly created a problem unique to the United States: the absence of legislative control over the powers delegated to bureaucrats.[26]

8

Those who hold this point of view assert that parliamentary systems are free from the inefficient administration, poorly formed programs, and unfulfilled legislative responsibilities caused by the American political system because members of parliamentary legislatures, unlike members of Congress, are responsible for choosing executive officials.[27] In the American system, these critics argue, congressional delegation of authority demoralizes and corrupts democratic government by making American citizens "lose control over the laws that govern them."[28] In addition, it undermines representation by encouraging members of Congress to dodge their lawmaking responsibilities, and magnifies the unintended consequences of government action by forcing administrators to implement poorly defined programs.[29]

Included among students of American administrative capacities who blame policy failures on constitutional structure is a group that focuses on the opposite kind of problem. Rather than pointing to the overabundance of discretionary authorities placed in the hands of bureaucrats, it claims that American administrative agencies are impotent because they are caught between two bosses. Agencies are built into the executive branch, and thus responsible to the president. But they are at the same time responsible to Congress, since they were created by it and are continually dependent on it for reauthorizations and annual appropriations.

This critique of the weakness of American bureaucratic authority concludes that the federal government is incapable of producing coherent solutions to social problems. Noting that the United States is the advanced industrial democratic country that has most room for improvement in meeting domestic welfare needs through public provision, it attributes the country's "relatively paltry public social programs" to a governmental structure that discourages unified, persistent policy implementation.[30] In other words, having been established through the congressional delegation of authority, American administrative agencies are inherently flawed and can produce little else than "a politics distinguished by incoherence and fragmentation in governmental operations and by the absence of clear lines of authoritative control."[31]

With respect to leadership capacities, the Wilsonian understanding finds expression today in the view that American government is doomed to "gridlock" and "deadlock."[32] Not surprisingly, therefore, President Nixon, who was intent on implementing his policies in spite of his ideological opponents dominating Congress, proclaimed himself a devotee of Woodrow Wilson. In line with Wilson's prescriptions for improving American politics, Nixon attempted to overcome policy stalemate by subordinating congressional policymaking prerogatives to executive administrative powers.[33]

But the Wilsonian framework has also appealed to those who have objected to such attempts to overcome interbranch gridlock. These critics blame the problems associated with an "Imperial Presidency," including the failed war in Vietnam and the Watergate scandal in particular, on an overreaching of presidential power that could not be restrained by Congress. For them, the formal separation between executive and legislative power is to blame for Congress's inability to retain control over the extraordinary powers delegated to the president in response to two world wars and the Great Depression.[34]

Thanks to the influence of the Wilsonian critique of the separation of powers, a critique cemented into the very foundations of contemporary political analysis, the legislative veto received a great deal more attention than it deserved. The myth of the legislative veto, in other words, had its roots in the Wilsonian mischaracterization of the principles of American constitutionalism. Operating within a Wilsonian framework, many students of American politics wrongly attributed great policymaking power to the legislative veto because they assumed that without it, Congress would be unable to exercise control over the administrative powers built into the executive branch in the twentieth century.[35] In addition, since they presumed that the emergence of a strong presidency was contrary to the spirit of the Constitution, they mistakenly expected legislative veto authority to free Congress from shackles that had supposedly prevented it from reacting against presidential power.[36]

These mistaken expectations reflect the ways in which the Wilsonian framework underestimates the great breadth and flexibility of power granted to Congress and to the presidency by the Constitution. With respect to the capacity of Congress to retain control over delegated authorities, the Wilsonian framework allowed legislative veto analysts to ignore the myriad procedural and institutional changes that accompanied the growth of administrative power in the executive branch. For example, members have proven capable of exercising strict control over policy implementation by drafting extremely detailed statutes.[37] In addition, as courts have become increasingly tangled up in determining the ways in which agencies exercise their administrative powers, warnings about unaccountable bureaucrats wielding unlimited regulatory powers have rung increasingly hollow.[38]

At the same time, the decentralization of Congress—requiring executive branch officials to communicate with a much larger number of members in building support for executive branch policies and budget requests—has helped broaden congressional participation in decisions about the implementation of policy.[39] Most importantly, legislative veto advocates who worried that Congress was structurally incapable of retaining control over delegated authorities overlooked the fact that the United States Congress is, after all, the most powerful legislature in the world.[40] Precisely because the separation of powers makes members of Congress electorally independent from the executive, Congress is much freer than parliamentary legislatures to exercise control over the policymaking activities of administrators.[41]

The Wilsonian framework also led legislative veto scholars to avoid exploring how the separation of powers system is consistent with, and well suited to accommodate, the growing aggregation of foreign policymaking power in the presidency. Congress has consistently exhibited a powerful impulse, throughout the postwar period, to remain, on one hand, informed and consulted about proposed foreign affairs activities and, on the other, to leave executive branch officials with the discretion and responsibility necessary for making final decisions.

The evolution of these congressional preferences has been hidden behind members' symbolic actions that have often made Congress seem deeply frustrated by constitutional restraints on its power to control foreign policy.[42] But understanding such rhetorical devices for what they are reveals that members have extensive powers—which they often prefer not to use—to control the foreign policymaking activities of the presidency. This understanding, in turn, reinforces the fact that the strong modern presidency is not, as the Wilsonian framework presumes, extra-constitutional.[43]

In this book, I place the legislative veto in a more appropriate framework for studying American political institutions. I do this, in part, by exploring the source of the misleading assumptions underlying the Wilsonian approach to constitutional analysis. In his famous critique of constitutional structure, Wilson asserted that the separation of powers was designed solely to restrain governmental authority by dividing it into separate institutions empowered to check each other. But the Framers also chose a tripartite system as a way of enhancing the capacity of government to simultaneously perform a variety of functions. By institutionally separating executive, legislative, and judicial powers, the Framers intended not only to encourage members of each branch to check the powers of the other branches, but also to produce a division of labor so that members of the different branches would develop specialized skills in pursuing the responsibilities of legislating, executing, and judging.

This understanding of the separation of powers—one that appreciates the power of separation—comes from the *Federalist Papers,* which explain how the constitutional order allows for flexibility in the balance of power among the three branches at the same time that it preserves the independent capacity of each of them to fulfill its particular tasks. From this point of view, the legislative veto does not immediately appear as a key instrument of congressional oversight. Already endowed with extensive powers with which to check and balance each other, members of the different branches are likely to produce a slew of counterbalancing mechanisms to any new powers that actually threaten to affect policy outcomes. From this point of view, too, the legislative veto acquires a potential political significance that is overlooked by conventional wisdom. As a shortcut through separation of powers procedures, the mechanism might weaken the capacity of legislators and administrators to do their different jobs well.

I begin with an analysis of the *Federalist Papers* because understanding the Framers' objectives illuminates the shortcomings of the conventional twentieth-century view of the separation of powers, and sheds light on the weaknesses inherent in many contemporary approaches to the study of American political institutions. After studying these weaknesses, I provide a more accurate account of the origins and development of the legislative veto mechanism than is possible within the confines of a Wilsonian framework. Then, in case studies of the legislative vetoes governing the Federal Trade Commission, the Department of Education, and the granting of most-favored-nation status, I analyze the history and development of public policy under each of the relevant statutes with particular attention to the shifting balance of policymaking powers between political institutions. Through this analysis, I identify the actual role played by the legislative veto mechanism, as well as the relative importance of other congressional control tools employed by members of Congress.

In so doing, I demonstrate that the legislative veto shortcut was inconsequential to congressional control of the policymaking process because of the extensive set of powers in the Constitution already available to members of Congress. In addition, the evidence of the case studies shows that the Supreme Court's restoration of separation of powers procedures (through invalidation of the legislative veto) in fact enhanced the capacity of Congress to fulfill representative functions and of the executive branch to carry out its executive responsibilities. It made it easier for members of Congress to pass laws containing substantive policy prescriptions at the same time that it made it easier for them to leave in the executive branch discretionary power to address the unpredictable demands and details of policy implementation.

In sum, this study of the legislative veto shows the disadvantages of the Wilsonian legacy in the study of American politics, a legacy that still constitutes the core of the political science discipline in the United States. The Wilsonian enthusiasm for overcoming the separation of powers must itself be overcome because it obscures the actual workings of American political institutions and the principles on which those institutions are based.

Chapter Two

THE AMERICAN SEPARATION OF POWERS DOCTRINE

For much of this century, many political scientists, legal scholars, and journalists have taken for granted that the eighteenth-century principles underlying the constitutional separation of powers are incompatible with the governing demands of the twentieth century.[1] They view "governmental inefficiency" as the inevitable cost of the Founding Fathers' "passion" for dividing power, "for setting ambition against ambition, for creating a constitution with a complicated system of balances exceeding that of any other."[2] With this understanding of the separation of powers as a mechanical system of checks and balances, described by Woodrow Wilson as a "copy of the Newtonian theory of the universe," these critics assert that the American political system is ill-suited to foster good administration.[3]

But this view mischaracterizes the actual principles of American constitutionalism. A careful re-examination of the origins and the classic elaboration of the American separation of powers doctrine demonstrates that constitutional structure embodies a dual commitment to ensuring effective governance as well as to protecting liberty. By misdirecting students of contemporary American politics to overlook this duality of objectives, the flawed, Wilsonian understanding of the separation of powers leads analysts to inaccurate conclusions about the dynamics of the policymaking process.

THE SEPARATION OF POWERS DOCTRINE

RE-EXAMINING THE SEPARATION OF POWERS DOCTRINE

When the Continental Congress was first created in 1774, it tried to carry out administrative duties by delegating executive powers to committees of its own members. In its earliest years, then, "Congress was primarily itself the executive, the administrator."[4] But this system soon caused a "general administrative debacle" that resulted in members of Congress demanding a "personal separation of powers" between themselves and those responsible for carrying out executive functions.[5] As a result, departments run by single executives were established in 1781. Well before the Constitutional Convention in 1787, therefore, "a separate executive had emerged for practical reasons in [the] search for greater governmental efficiency."[6]

Practical experience also led George Washington to favor the institutional separation of executive and legislative powers. As commander in chief of the American Revolutionary War forces, he suffered daily from Congress's failure to carry out administrative functions. So he was keenly aware of the "well known" fact that "the impotence of Congress under the former confederation, and the inexpediency of trusting more ample prerogatives to a single Body, gave birth to the different branches which constitute the present general government."[7]

Even the opponents of the new Constitution, the Anti-Federalists, believed that "to have a government well administered in all its parts, it is requisite the different departments of it should be separated."[8] Theorists of constitutional structure since Aristotle, in fact, have observed that different governing responsibilities are best fulfilled by different types of institutions.[9] The manifestation of this view in the new Constitution is most obvious in the analysis of executive and judicial power articulated by Publius in the *Federalist Papers*.[10]

To define executive power, Publius contrasts it to legislative power. Legislative power is necessarily plural since "deliberation and wisdom" in the legislative process demand "a numerous legislature."[11] Executive power, however, characterized by "energy" to engage in "decision, activity, secrecy, and dispatch," must be unitary. Since "energy in the executive is a leading character in the definition of good government," Publius chooses a separation of powers system in order to endow the new government with the unitary executive necessary for exercising executive power energetically.[12] He separates executive and legislative power, in other words, to foster the specialization that comes from a division of labor.

Similarly, when analyzing judicial power, Publius describes the tripartite constitutional system as one that will make government better at fulfilling its varied responsibilities. Without a separate judiciary, it would be impossible to make judicial power independent from electoral pressures. Such independence is necessary, according to Publius, to ensure the competence of judges. Otherwise, those best skilled in the law would be unlikely to "[quit] a lucrative line of practice to accept a seat on the bench."[13] As a result, the administration of justice would be thrown "into hands less able and less well qualified to conduct it with utility and dignity."[14] By placing judicial power in an institution independent from the other branches, the new Constitution could provide judges with life tenure and thereby attract the best candidates.

Clearly, Publius expects the separation of powers system to foster particular institutional competences in the exercise of "the several classes of power, as they may in their nature be legislative, executive, or judiciary."[15] But he resists those who would demand pure distinctions in the "nature" of different types of political powers, noting: "Experience has instructed us that no skill in the science of government has yet been able to discriminate and define, with sufficient certainty, its three great provinces—the legislative, executive, and judiciary."[16]

Indeed, promoting a division of labor in the exercise of governmental powers was not the only objective that led Publius to choose a tripartite system. By the time the Framers arrived in Philadelphia for the convention in 1787, theorists of liberal constitutionalism had already agreed that the separation of powers was necessary for protecting individual liberty. Both Montesquieu and Locke had "placed great stress on the separation of powers as a requisite for a rule of law in the public interest."[17] Montesquieu analyzed governmental power as consisting of three categories, explaining that "all would be lost if the same man or the same body of principal men, either of nobles, or of the people, exercised these three powers: that of making the laws, that of executing public resolutions, and that of judging the crimes or the disputes of individuals."[18]

THE SEPARATION OF POWERS DOCTRINE

The Anti-Federalists attacked the tripartite structure in the proposed Constitution because they considered it untrue to Montesquieu's theory. They believed that the Constitution did not keep the three powers separated enough. It placed in the Senate, for example, an

> undue and dangerous mixture of the powers of government; the same body possessing legislative, executive, and judicial powers. The senate is a constituent branch of the legislature, it has judicial power in judging on impeachments. . . . And the senate has, moreover, various and great executive powers, viz. in concurrence with the president-general, they form treaties with foreign nations, that may controul and abrogate the constitutions and laws of the several states.[19]

"Montesquieu," they argued, would have seen "such various, extensive, and important powers combined in one body of men, [as] inconsistent with all freedom."[20]

Publius responded to these vociferous objections by claiming that he had looked to "the celebrated Montesquieu" as his "oracle" on how to structure governmental powers.[21] Publius acknowledged that the Constitution seemed to violate the political maxim that the legislative, executive and judiciary departments ought to be separate and distinct, noting the Anti-Federalist complaint that in the structure of the new federal government "no regard, it is said, seems to have been paid to this essential precaution in favor of liberty."[22] But he defended himself by explaining that his separation of powers system would be better at preventing threatening concentrations of power in any one institution than a system that kept the formal powers more purely separated.

Publius argued that a "partial mixture" of the three governmental powers would provide the "necessary constitutional means and personal motives to resist encroachments of the others."[23] In contrast, a pure separation of powers system—the kind demanded by the Anti-Federalists—would provide no protective weapons to enable members of each branch to check potential abuses of members in the other branches. Without a mixture of powers within each branch, Publius warned, constitutional provisions expressly prohibiting the encroachment of one branch on another would prove nothing more than "parchment barriers."[24]

The Anti-Federalist attack on the new Constitution forced Publius to emphasize the contribution that the new government's separation of powers system would make to political liberty. Consequently, he devoted relatively little attention to the other benefits he expected the system to produce—specifically, the more effective governance that would result from an institutional division of labor. Thus, it could seem that the Framers' sole intention in separating powers and institutionalizing checks was to protect liberty by preventing unwanted exercises of those powers. But this emphasis reflected the political needs of the moment, not the whole reasoning behind the tripartite governmental structure.

The Wilsonian Misunderstanding

Publius's emphasis on how the checks and balances would work in the new Constitution became key targets for the twentieth-century critique of the American political system originated by Woodrow Wilson. According to Wilson, the Federalists' attempt to institutionalize checks between the three branches had failed. Thus, "the noble charter of fundamental law given us by the Convention of 1787" had become "our *form of government* rather in name than in reality, the form of the Constitution being one of nicely adjusted, ideal balances, whilst the actual form of our present government is simply a scheme of congressional supremacy."[25]

From Wilson's point of view, the constitutional system of checks and balances had failed because societal changes by the end of the nineteenth century had produced a "centralization of governmental functions such as could not have suggested itself as a possibility to the framers of the Constitution."[26] This increasing centralization and expansion of federal powers made it impossible for the Constitution's interbranch checks to restrain the encroachment of congressional power. As a result, Congress became "the predominant and controlling force, the centre and source of all motive and of all regulative power."[27]

Yet, while Wilson blamed the constitutional checks as too weak to preserve the Framers' intended interbranch balance, he also blamed them for exercising harmful restraints on congressional power. By preventing Congress from retaining complete control over "its executive agencies," the separation of powers system deprived the legislature of its rightful authority.[28] Wilson criticized Congress for being too strong on the one hand, and too weak on the other, because the main thrust of his critique was not directed at Congress. It was directed at the mechanistic, "Newtonian" physics he attributed to the Constitution's tripartite structure. "As at present constituted," Wilson concluded, "the federal government lacks strength because its powers are divided, lacks promptness because its authorities are multiplied, lacks wieldiness because its processes are roundabout, lacks efficiency because its responsibility is indistinct and its action without competent direction."[29] Thus, while constitutional structure was too weak in the face of societal change to keep government organized as it had been in the nineteenth century, it was too resistant to allowing political institutions to overcome the system completely, as Wilson believed was necessary.

Careful study of the *Federalist Papers* reveals that Woodrow Wilson's conclusions rest on an incomplete understanding of the constitutional separation of powers. He focuses on Publius's famous response, in Papers #47–51, to the Anti-Federalist attack on the new Constitution's seemingly dangerous intermixture of powers. In that discussion of the three branches, Publius abstracts from the qualities of executive, legislative, and judicial power in order to concentrate on the branches' mutual checking capacities. It is in later Papers that Publius develops the "positive intention" of the tripartite system: "to contribute 'energy' and 'stability,' so as to constitute a 'good' or 'useful' government rather than merely a safe one."[32]

CONTEMPORARY RELEVANCE OF THE *FEDERALIST*'S PRINCIPLES

A sound understanding of the separation of powers doctrine illuminates the continuing relevance of Publius's political science because it crystallizes the central problem that Publius was trying to solve. The constitutional separation of powers is predicated on Publius's conviction that "framing a government which is to be administered by men over men" demands attention to fostering effective governance as well as to protecting liberty.[31] Government must be restrained from violating individual liberty, remaining "strictly republican" in deriving all of its powers from "the great body of the society, not from an inconsiderable proportion or a favored class of it";[32] and it must also encourage "firmness and efficiency" in the exercise of governmental power because "the true test of a good government is its aptitude and tendency to produce a good administration."[33]

Publius understood these principles to be in tension. So he admits that "combining the requisite stability and energy in government with the inviolable attention due to liberty and to the republican form . . . could not be easily accomplished."[34] But he is nonetheless firm in his conviction that both must be inscribed in the new Constitution. Publius's political science remains instructive to those who view this tension as worth preserving. And it remains provocative because Publius claims that in important ways, the dual objectives at stake—protecting the sovereignty of the people over their government, and fostering effective governance of the people—in fact depend upon each other in practice.

Thus, Publius argues that protecting the liberty and sovereignty of the people demands a powerful government capable of stable and competent administration. Otherwise, attempts at self-government will succumb to "sudden and violent passions," producing "instability, injustice, and confusion."[35] Publius draws on historical analysis to show that the failure to "blend stability with liberty" has proven the "mortal diseas[e] under which popular governments have everywhere perished."[36] He justifies the "energy" built into the independent executive, the "tenure of considerable duration" held by senators, and the "firmness of the judicial magistracy," by warning that "a dangerous ambition more often lurks behind the specious mask of zeal for the rights of the people than under the forbidding appearance of zeal for the firmness and efficiency of government."[37]

The capacity for good administration is itself dependent on protecting liberty and popular sovereignty, Publius adds, because "the people are the only legitimate fountain of power."[38] Thus, without "the prejudices of the community on its side," without the people's "confidence in the public councils," not even "the wisest and freest" nor "most rational government" is likely to possess the "requisite stability" to effectively develop and implement public policy.[39] No amount of centralized power, in other words, can enable government to sustain, over the long run, effective administration of policies that run counter to the "reason, justice, and truth . . . [of] the public mind."[40] But a robustly representative government, encouraging active participation of widely divergent interests, can provide government with the on-going information necessary to forge policies whose effective implementation will be encouraged rather than frustrated by those forced to comply with them.[41]

EMPIRICAL SHORTCOMINGS RESULTING FROM MISCHARACTERIZED CONSTITUTIONAL PRINCIPLES

By ignoring the ways in which the separation of powers system attempts to foster stable, well-reasoned administration at the same time that it seeks to protect liberty, the Wilsonian framework denies the contemporary relevance of Publius's political science. The Wilsonian view even appears among those who believe that the eighteenth-century Constitution should be preserved. In Justice Brandeis's view, "the doctrine of the separation of powers was adopted by the Convention of 1787, not to promote efficiency but to preclude the exercise of arbitrary power."[42] Brandeis's famous dictum continues to keep alive, in contemporary legal scholarship, the misleading presumption that the Framers ignored the demands of good governance. In the case of the legislative veto, this led supporters of the Framers' Constitution, including Chief Justice Burger, to accept the unexamined, and mistaken, assertion that the shortcut through constitutional procedure had enhanced Congress's control over delegated authorities.[43]

Clearly, Chief Justice Burger was not responsible for determining the practical significance of the veto mechanism in order to declare it unconstitutional. But he might at least have properly articulated the principles underlying the separation of powers system rather than assuming that constitutional structure is worth preserving for its own sake. Had he done so, explaining how the Framers expected the separation of powers to foster effective governance as well as to protect liberty, his opinion would have forced legislative veto scholars to question the widespread claim that the constitutional innovation was necessary to protect Congress's rightful place in the policymaking process.

More generally, mischaracterizations of the separation of powers doctrine have led students of American politics to shortsighted conclusions about the political system's working capacity for policy leadership and good administration. This is most evident in the arguments of those who explicitly call for constitutional changes to make American government more like a parliamentary system. True to the Wilsonian reform vision, Lloyd Cutler, one of the most prominent of these reformers, helped establish a Committee on the Constitutional System (CCS) in the mid-1980s (to coincide with the bicentennial of the Constitution) to explore how such changes would improve the policymaking process. A decade later, the CCS remained committed to the view that "the government needs to be empowered and liberated from a constitutional structure designed for another age."[44]

Cutler blames the separation of powers, for example, for President Carter's failure to enact the SALT II treaty. President Carter had successfully completed and signed the treaty, which "he and his cabinet regarded as very much in the national security interests of the United States," in 1979. But the national interest failed to be served, according to Cutler, because of the constitutional requirement for Senate approval of treaties. This failure of the system in the case of SALT II is "replicated regularly," in Cutler's view, "over the whole range of legislation required to carry out any president's overall program" because the constitutional requirement for a simple majority of both houses is at times "even more difficult than achieving a two-thirds vote in the Senate."[45]

Cutler's lament about the separation of powers is evident among a much wider group of scholars than the self-proclaimed constitutional reformers. In a more subtle and muted manner, the Wilsonian conviction that overabundant checks and balances are responsible for the ills of American politics has found its way into many seminal studies of the American political system. This even includes studies in the behavioral tradition, a tradition within the political science discipline that rejected the institutional focus of scholars such as Woodrow Wilson.

One of the most distinguished behavioral political scientists, Robert Dahl, in one of his most famous books, presents the Madisonian logic behind the constitutional separation of powers as an unfortunate exaggeration of the necessity for checks on governmental power.[46] It is unfortunate, according to Dahl, because it makes American political institutions unable to act in accordance with the requirements of democratic society. Dahl blames the "clearly inadequate" political science of the Madisonian system for wrongly inhibiting and limiting majorities. As such, he concludes that the separation of powers system makes political leaders ineffective at implementing the policies demanded by a majority of Americans because the political system is structurally riddled with veto points.[47]

Critics of contemporary American politics would not stop at constitutional structure to explain policy stalemate if they had a better understanding of Publius's political science.[48] Instead, sensitive to the tension embodied in the separation of powers between liberty and effectiveness, these critics would at least wonder whether the failure to enact particular proposals reflects a strength of the system rather than a weakness. They would look to see how such failures might have resulted from the successful representation of legitimate objections. And they would most certainly refrain from perpetuating the romanticized Wilsonian view of parliamentary government, a view that overlooks the costs of having executive and legislative powers fused in one institution.[49]

Lloyd Cutler, for example, would have questioned whether SALT II was indeed in the best interests of the nation.[50] Similarly, those who blamed the separation of powers for the Clinton administration's failure to enact comprehensive health care reform in 1994 would instead have explored the breadth and depth of public support for the particular program proposed by the administration.[51] Before concluding that the separation of powers is responsible for stalemate, furthermore, students of American politics would seek to complement their study of failed policy proposals with an explanation for why and how successful proposals received the majorities necessary for enactment.[52]

In addition, by keeping in mind the ways in which constitutional structure attempts to foster a division of labor between the branches, critics of the separation of powers would be compelled to examine more than just the weakness of the president's policymaking powers as compared to those of the prime minister in a parliamentary system. They would also explore the practical consequences of the president's uniquely broad executive prerogative powers.

The same structural separation between the president and Congress that can make it relatively difficult for the president to receive legislative support for his policy proposals also frees the president to become extremely powerful at critical moments that demand immediate, and potentially unpopular, governmental action.[53] Having learned this as commander in chief of the American armed forces during World War I, Woodrow Wilson himself brought into question the analysis of American constitutional structure he had articulated as a political scientist. As a war president, Wilson "took refuge in the Founders' Constitution, invoking the prerogatives that the document vested upon him as commander in chief and using to the fullest the insulated position that most distinguishes the American presidency from other chief executives."[54] As critic of the analytical framework his own scholarship exemplified, Wilson concluded that "our present form of government was the best in time of war. This was indicated by the fluidity of the situations developing and overturning the cabinets on the other side; whereas, ours was compact all the time."[55]

Those who take the constitutional sanction of a strong president to an extreme make themselves as vulnerable to shortsighted evaluations of American government as those who ignore the uniquely powerful character of the American executive altogether. This pro-executive variety of the Wilsonian critique calls upon the presidency to deny members of Congress their independent authority to demand consultation on, and oversight of, executive branch actions.[56] But this view wrongly presumes that such congressional authority is inevitably contrary to the interests of effective execution of public policy.

Indeed, a sound education in Publius's political science would lead advocates of executive prerogative to explore how the successful use of presidential power is, in the long run, dependent upon receiving the kind of broad support necessary for enacting legislation.[57] In addition, such well-informed analysts would seek to complement their critique of counterproductive "congressional micromanagement" with an examination of the conditions under which congressional oversight of administration results in more, rather than less, effective governance.[58]

Mischaracterizations of the separation of powers doctrine also appear to skew the conclusions of those who study the evolution of American administrative capacities. Most importantly, Theodore Lowi's influential study of open-ended delegations of congressional authority blames the discretionary powers placed in the hands of bureaucrats as the source of governance failures. Such delegations are unworkable, Lowi argues, because they are incompatible with constitutional structure. Without clear policy direction from the legislature, broad grants of authority to administrators in the American separation of powers system necessarily result in "an imposition of impotence." According to Lowi, government inevitably becomes impotent in the face of democratic demands because American administrative authorities cannot produce the broad statutory statements necessary to establish new policy directions. Administrators can only use their delegated powers to respond, piecemeal, to the demands of particular interest groups. In so doing, they violate the values of representative governance.[59]

More recent scholarship in the growing field of Positive Political Theory (PPT), a field devoted to theoretical analysis of inter-institutional dynamics, echoes Lowi's conclusions. PPT scholarship models the Framers as having created a system where political outcomes would be the "creatures of an 'equilibrium'" between the executive, legislative, and judicial branches.[60] These models, in turn, presume that the creation of administrative agencies, endowing bureaucrats with discretionary policymaking authorities, has undermined the original balance of power among the branches. Like Lowi, PPT scholarship understands the delegation of congressional authority characteristic of the twentieth century as structurally incompatible with the proper functioning of the separation of powers system.[61]

Were they to keep in mind that in the separation of powers system, the objectives of good administration and proper representation are at times interdependent, scholars who share Lowi's perspective would be forced to temper their criticism. They would not overlook those cases in which the delegation of congressional authority serves the demands of both values.[62] They would need to explore how certain agencies have succeeded in acquiring widespread respect as "effective" implementers of public policy, and how the delegation of discretionary powers to such agencies has been produced and protected by explicit, on-going, broad-based congressional consensus.[63] And perhaps most importantly, before concluding that costly governance failures are irreversible, critics of the American political system would explore the ways in which the separation of powers encourages the restructuring, or even elimination, of poorly administered public policies.[64]

Contemporary students of American government operating within a Wilsonian framework would be much more likely to recognize its limits if they knew more about its source. Unlike his intellectual descendants, Woodrow Wilson would not have disputed the charge that his political science was empirically flawed. For Wilson was first and foremost a reformer. Persuading the American people to reform their political institutions was more important to Wilson than providing the best empirical analyses of these institutions. His scholarly work was dedicated to furthering his partisan objectives, not to exploring the actual strengths and weaknesses of the existing constitutional order.

Indeed, Wilson admonished his scholarly colleagues not to name their discipline "political science." In his presidential address to the recently founded American Political Science Association, he explained his reasons for preferring the title "politics": "Human relationships . . . are not in any proper sense the subject-matter of science. . . . I prefer the term Politics, therefore, to include both the statesmanship of thinking and the statesmanship of action. . . . Know your people and you can lead them; study your people and you may know them."[65]

To best serve his reform ends, Wilson presented his ideological convictions with seeming objectivity and scientific rigor. In his *Congressional Government,* the most influential expression of the view that the separation of powers is impractical and the cause of dysfunction, Wilson dispassionately described weaknesses of the presidential-congressional system in comparison to strengths of the British parliamentary system. But his goal was resolutely political. He hoped to fuel a "great national movement for reform of the American governmental system through a modified adoption of the [British] Cabinet system."[66] Thus, he found it unnecessary to travel to Washington, D.C., to observe Congress at first hand because he intended his study to serve political movements, not objective standards of scientific inquiry.[67] As he himself explained:

> If ever any book was written with fulness and earnestness of conviction, with purpose of imparting conviction, [*Congressional Government*] was. . . . Its mission was to *stir* thought and to carry irresistible practical suggestion, and it was as such a missionary that it carried my hopes and ambitions with it. I carefully kept all advocacy of particular reforms out of it, because I wanted it to be . . . a permanent piece of work, not a political pamphlet, which couldn't succeed without destroying its own reason for being; but I hoped at the same time that it might catch hold of its readers' convictions and set reform a-going in a very definite direction.[68]

The following chapters re-examine the legislative veto controversy in light of the everyday workings of American political institutions. Once freed from the blinders of the Wilsonian framework, students of American government can see the power of the separation of powers system, a system that not only checks government action, but also fosters institutional adaptation and reversibility, promotes the enactment of substantive laws that rest on broad-based consensus, and protects the capacity for energetic exercise of executive power.

Chapter Three
THE LEGISLATIVE VETO

Harold Koh, a professor at Yale Law School, tells of the night he and some of his fellow Supreme Court clerks happened to be discussing legal issues as they were waiting in line to rent a movie at a video store. When it came time for them to pay for the movie, the attendant at the cash register asked them in somewhat hushed tones, and with an Indian accent, "Are you law students?" Upon their replying yes, the attendant broke into a grand smile, pointed at himself, then raised his arms in victory, and declared, "I am Chadha!"[1]

Jagdish Chadha, the man who filed the suit that ultimately resulted in the 1983 Supreme Court decision that struck down the legislative veto as unconstitutional, might very well have asked Harold Koh and his friends if they were political scientists or journalists. The *Chadha* decision attracted widespread attention from analysts of American politics because it invalidated a legislative review procedure that was perceived to have enhanced congressional control over policymaking.[2] Many analysts continue to view the veto mechanism as a significant instrument of congressional power since members of Congress seem to have flouted the Supreme Court's decision by continuing to enact and exercise legislative veto authority.[3] The reams of paper devoted by political scientists, journalists, and legal scholars to the implications and consequences of the Supreme Court's decision resulted from the view that, for good or for ill, "the legislative veto was the most forceful continuing expression of the congressional resurgence" against executive power that began in the early 1970s.[4]

Tracing the political controversies that grew up around the legislative veto shows that there was good reason why analysts of American politics expected it to have profound consequences for the balance of power between the branches. But empirical analysis of the veto provisions that were actually enacted into law reveals that these expectations were ill-founded. These expectations overlooked the extensive oversight powers, all perfectly constitutional, possessed by Congress. These expectations also exaggerated the capacity of the legislative veto to actually affect policy outcomes. To determine the real political significance of the innovative constitutional shortcut requires empirical analysis that, unlike existing studies, is free of distorted assumptions about how the separation of powers system works. Most importantly, it demands that scholars reject the mistaken assumption that the constitutional system restricts Congress's policymaking power solely to the formal authority to pass laws.

THE POLITICS OF THE LEGISLATIVE VETO'S CONSTITUTIONALITY

The majority in *Chadha* invalidated the legislative veto based on a straightforward reading of the constitutional requirements for legislative action.[5] The legislative veto was unconstitutional, Chief Justice Burger reasoned, because it authorized members of Congress to bypass the bicameralism and presentment clauses of Article I.[6]

But to Justice White, the legislative veto was a welcome example of constitutional evolution. The extraordinary twentieth-century growth in "the complexity and size of the Federal Government's responsibilities" had made the legislative veto, in White's mind, "the most effective if not the only means to insure [Congress's] role as the Nation's lawmaker."[7] Without the legislative veto, White claimed,

> Congress is faced with a Hobson's choice: either to refrain from delegating the necessary authority, leaving itself with a hopeless task of writing laws with the requisite specificity to cover endless special circumstances across the entire policy landscape, or in the alternative, to abdicate its lawmaking function to the Executive Branch and independent agencies. To choose the former leaves major national problems unresolved; to opt for the latter risks unaccountable policymaking by those not elected to fill that role.[8]

White objected to the majority opinion because it invalidated the legislative veto even though the mechanism was an "important if not indispensable political invention."[9]

Underlying White's dissent was a deep objection to the strictly formalist grounds on which the majority invalidated the legislative veto. Functionalists object to the willingness to "sacrifice the goal of a workable government in favor of a strict and formalistic interpretation of separation of powers."[10] The focus of their approach is, in contrast, on "the need for flexibility in separation of powers doctrine and the declaration that courts should not reach out unnecessarily to decide separation of powers issues."[11] *Chadha* is a perfect example of the sort of decision that functionalists find objectionable because "its holding that the veto is unconstitutional [did] not turn upon any fact concerning the veto's origin, its purposes, or its balance of power effects. Rather, the decision . . . [was] based upon the language of the Constitution, upon its structural dictates, not upon the function of the veto."[12]

Though Justice Burger and Justice White held diametrically opposed convictions about the proper approach to separation of powers jurisprudence, together they echoed and encouraged the conventional view of the veto mechanism as a powerful policymaking instrument. This faulty presumption resonated with the beliefs of many political scientists, legal scholars, and journalists because they had long viewed the legislative veto as a valuable antidote to weaknesses in the political system that they attributed to the constitutional structure. Though critiques of the separation of powers take a wide variety of forms, they converge in blaming the tripartite system for making Congress incapable of properly overseeing administration.[13] Consequently, many analysts viewed the legislative veto as "one of the most significant institutional developments in twentieth-century American politics" because it endowed Congress with extra-constitutional controls over delegated authorities.[14]

Burger's majority opinion corroborated this conventional wisdom by supporting Justice White's view of the legislative veto as a functional solution to governmental needs. The majority did not question Justice White's claim that the veto was an "indispensable political invention" or that "it has become a central means by which Congress secures the accountability of executive and independent agencies."[15] Quite to the contrary. They stated rather bluntly that "we need not challenge" Justice White's "utilitarian argument."[16] And they asserted that "the fact that a given law or procedure is efficient, convenient,

29

and useful in facilitating functions of government . . . will not save it if it is contrary to the Constitution."[17]

The conventional view of the legislative veto as a powerful instrument of congressional control was also dominant among scholars and commentators who opposed its enactment into law.[18] Many of them deemed the *Chadha* decision a welcome reaction against the corrosive effects of "congressional imperialism." They believed that the legislative veto reflected an "insatiable [congressional] appetite" for exercising executive branch powers.[19] They expected its elimination to stop Congress from "second guess[ing] and rework[ing]" policies proposed by the president and executive branch agencies.[20] Thus, by presuming that the legislative veto played an important role in determining the balance of policymaking power between the branches, these analysts could describe *Chadha* as one of the executive branch's "successful counterattacks against the tyranny of special interests."[21]

The legislative veto's seeming capacity to enhance congressional oversight powers was especially noteworthy in an era of interbranch acrimony. The Supreme Court's invalidation of the veto mechanism, which came during the first years of the "Congress-bashing" Reagan administration, followed a decade of divided government in which Republicans usually controlled the White House and Democrats controlled Congress. Thus, those who believed that constitutional structure already imposed too many limits on legislative power criticized the Supreme Court for having a Republican bias that made Congress "the one branch of the Federal Government that most often ends up," in separation of powers cases, "on the short end of the stick."[22]

The reason the legislative veto landed in court, in fact, is a direct result of the interbranch hostility that arose between the Republicans in the executive branch and the Democrats in Congress in the early 1970s. Since the inception of the veto mechanism in the 1930s, members of Congress had been well aware of its questionable constitutionality. This uncertainty made many members skeptical of the mechanism's value, so they enacted it only sporadically, into a small number of statutes. But their newfound commitment to re-establishing congressional control over policymaking in the early 1970s led them to challenge those who deemed the legislative veto illegitimate. Indeed, one member referred to the legislative veto issue as one of the most explicit examples of Congress choosing to "ignore the Constitution." Faced with legal opinions that alerted Congress to the mechanism's constitutional infirmities, members chose to enact it into law anyway because they "decided that the legislative veto was more important than any constitutional questions."[23]

As members became more enamored of enacting legislative veto provisions into law, they called upon the Congressional Research Service (CRS) to keep track of these enactments. Members then used these lists of provisions as growing evidence of the mechanism's indispensability. They believed that such evidence was tantamount to proving the legislative veto's constitutionality. Noting that "an adverse ruling by the Supreme Court may affect over 160 statutes, many of which are very significant laws," Rep. Elliott Levitas (D-GA) assured his colleagues that the Supreme Court was not very likely to declare the legislative veto unconstitutional.[24]

At the same time that members of Congress began to cite the growing number of legislative veto provisions as proof of the mechanism's constitutionality, officials in the Justice Department and the White House began to pay attention to the same phenomenon for exactly the opposite reason. Executive branch officials viewed the exponential growth in the number of veto provisions as evidence that the new mechanism was an unconstitutional congressional obsession. "We began, in the 1970s, to track the numbers of legislative vetoes enacted every year," one staff attorney from the Justice Department's Office of Legal Counsel (OLC) recalled, "as part of our strategy to land the legislative veto in court and have it declared unconstitutional."[25]

Every attorney general had objected to the legislative veto on constitutional grounds since William Mitchell advised President Hoover not to sign the 1933 Reorganization Act.[26] Some presidents had at times vetoed bills because they contained such provisions. At other times, presidents had signed bills containing legislative vetoes but had simultaneously issued strong statements that they would not pay heed to the legislative veto provisions.[27] By the mid-1970s, however, the explosion in the numbers of legislative vetoes inserted in bills made these responses either infeasible or useless.[28] So "the Justice Department decided that the time had come for a judicial showdown on their long-argued contention that the legislative veto violated the Constitution."[29]

When the Ninth Circuit Court declared the legislative veto unconstitutional in *Chadha v INS* (1980),[30] the Justice Department saw it as "a promising case" with which to attack the legislative veto on appeal to the Supreme Court.[31] At issue in the Circuit Court case was the constitutionality of the legislative veto in the Immigration and Naturalization Act (INA) of 1952. This "one-house veto" allowed either chamber of Congress to nullify decisions of the attorney general to suspend deportations. Jagdish Chadha, a native of Kenya and holder of a British passport, had entered the United States lawfully on a student visa that expired in 1972. Once the INS began deportation proceedings in 1974, Chadha conceded his deportable status. He requested and was granted a suspension of deportation, however, in 1974.[32] Soon thereafter, the House passed a veto resolution, without debate or recorded vote, disapproving some of the deportation suspensions submitted by the attorney general in 1974.[33] As a result, the INS was required, by law, to deport Chadha back to Kenya.[34]

The Ninth Circuit Court found this one-house veto to have unlawfully placed in Congress the typical day-to-day law enforcement functions of the executive. The legislative veto had also violated the principle of bicameralism by enacting positive law without the concurrence of both houses of Congress.[35] The significance of these infractions was compounded by the fact that they resulted in the violation of Chadha's liberties. He was denied the right to stay in the country even though he had appealed for and received such authority from the attorney general. "'When I heard about the veto,' Chadha remembers, 'I just knew it was wrong. I went to the local law school library and read everything I could find about the constitutional concept of fairness.'"[36]

The Ninth Circuit Court's *Chadha* decision both worried and appealed to those in the Justice Department intent on having the Supreme Court strike down the legislative veto. One of the OLC lawyers who had worked on the legislative veto issue since the early 1970s explained that the case was attractive, on the one hand, because

> it was blatantly obvious that the House had suspended Chadha's deportation for no reason. This case made it very clear that violating the separation of powers could lead to precisely the sort of tyranny that the Framers intended to guard against when they set up a variety of procedural requirements for legislative action. If there was any case in which the Supreme Court would strike down the legislative veto as unconstitutional, it seemed most likely to be this one.[37]

On the other hand, the injustice evident in Chadha's deportation threatened to divert the Supreme Court's attention away from the legislative veto controversy.[38] Lawyers in the Justice Department worried that the Supreme Court's review of the Ninth Circuit Court's decision would "just invalidate the INA veto and stop at that. But we wanted the Court to help us stop Congress from enacting legislative vetoes in foreign policy statutes and in statutes governing the authorities of administrative agencies."[39]

Much to the chagrin of those intent on expanding congressional prerogative with legislative veto authority, the Justice Department ultimately got its way. The Supreme Court used the Ninth Circuit Court's *Chadha* decision as the basis for its ruling on the constitutionality of the veto mechanism. And it did not restrict the scope of its decision to the particular legislative veto at issue in the INA.[40] The Supreme Court's decision, Justice Powell noted at the time, "apparently will invalidate every use of the legislative veto. The breadth of this holding gives one pause."[41] The great scope of the Supreme Court's decision, Justice White noticed, meant that it had struck down, "in one fell swoop provisions in more laws enacted by Congress than the Court has cumulatively invalidated in its history."[42] To those partisans of congressional prerogative who had been tracking the numbers of legislative veto provisions enacted every year, the Supreme Court's *Chadha* ruling was a "statute-shattering"[43] decision that "affected our government as few decisions have or ever will."[44]

One political scientist went so far as to claim that the loss of the legislative veto had helped make the Reagan administration successful at dominating Congress. In contrast to Carter, who had operated "in an era of congressional ascendancy," Reagan faced "an entirely different climate" that was partly due to the fact that "within two years of his election, the Supreme Court had declared the legislative veto unconstitutional."[45]

But the legislative veto struck down by the Supreme Court was not nearly as essential in enhancing members' capacities to control policymaking as the rhetoric surrounding it led conventional wisdom to believe. Empirical analysis of *Chadha*'s precise legal effect on the statutes containing legislative veto provisions, combined with a broad overview of the political consequences of these legal changes, point to two unexamined assumptions that plague this conventional wisdom. The more obvious of these two problems grows out of the exaggeration of the actual scope of the decision. By underestimating the breadth and flexibility of the oversight powers possessed by Congress, scholars and commentators assumed that *Chadha* had tainted all of the congressional control procedures that had accumulated under the "legislative veto" banner over the years.

33

Secondly, existing scholarship fails to question whether the mechanism ever played a significant role in affecting policy outcomes. Even Justice White failed to demand such a study, though his reasoning relied on a "functional" analysis of the constitutional invention under investigation.

THE SCOPE OF *CHADHA*

The Supreme Court deemed legislative vetoes unconstitutional because they formally empowered Congress to bypass the bicameralism and presentment requirements. Most debates about the importance and functions of the "legislative veto," however, included other congressional oversight mechanisms that did not violate these procedures. Most importantly, almost all descriptions, tabulations, and discussions of the legislative veto throughout the 1970s and early 1980s included "report-and-wait" provisions.[46] But such provisions simply require the executive to report proposed actions to Congress before implementing them. With such a broad definition of "legislative veto," it was perhaps to be expected that many analysts of American politics would mistakenly interpret *Chadha* to portend great functional problems.

The Supreme Court aggravated these worries by asserting, without much explanation, that Congress cannot act outside constitutionally prescribed legislative procedures. It declared that "Congress must abide by its delegation of authority until that delegation is legislatively altered or revoked."[47] By avoiding any discussion of the functions and objectives that the legislative veto was supposed to achieve, the majority decision in *Chadha* left open the possibility that congressional oversight control itself was constitutionally suspect.[48] Chief Justice Burger's "rigid and mechanical"[49] reasoning did not make clear whether the Supreme Court was "merely disapproving of the manner in which Congress chose to" achieve the ends the legislative veto was supposed to achieve, or whether it was "invalidating" the ends themselves.[50] Consequently, many analysts believed that *Chadha* would deal a crippling blow to congressional oversight power.[51]

Among those who mistakenly allowed the term "legislative veto" to include all kinds of activities that violated neither the bicameralism nor the presentment clauses was Rep. Claude Pepper (D-FL). He worried that the Supreme Court's invalidation of the legislative veto prohibited Congress from engaging in legislative oversight. To assuage this worry, he called upon his colleagues in Congress to continue enacting veto provisions into law so that the Supreme Court would be forced to deal with "case after case" of challenges to the majority opinion in *Chadha*.[52] But his colleagues viewed such a strategy as unnecessary. They understood that the Supreme Court's invalidation of the legislative veto was unlikely to influence the informal relationships between the branches that characterize the process of everyday governing. In direct response to Pepper's worries, Rep. Gillis W. Long (D-LA) noted that congressional instruments for overseeing the activities of administrative agencies, consisting mainly of informal interbranch contacts, had not "really [been] affected . . . at all" by the Supreme Court's insistence on upholding the bicameralism and presentment clauses.[53]

Had Rep. Pepper paid more careful attention to the separation of powers analysis underlying the Supreme Court's invalidation of the legislative veto, he would not have been as concerned about protecting congressional prerogative. In defining the constitutional infirmities of the legislative veto, the Supreme Court clearly distinguished it from report-and-wait provisions. Reporting provisions provide Congress with the opportunity to analyze proposed executive action, and to badger an agency with extensive questions or threats if the proposed action is somehow unsatisfactory. But they do not allow Congress to overturn that proposed action, or threaten to overturn it, by a process that shortcuts the full legislative process. The Supreme Court asserted that report-and-wait is constitutional because it does not provide members with the formal authority to "unilaterally veto" any set of proposed actions. "Rather, it [gives] Congress the opportunity to review the Rules before they [become] effective and to pass legislation barring their effectiveness if the Rules [are] found objectionable."[54]

The Supreme Court's distinction between report-and-wait provisions and legislative vetoes means that congressional oversight mechanisms are legitimate as long as they rely solely on informal political pressures or a threat to re-engage the full legislative process. In practice, members' ability to exercise informal pressures on administrators, often forcing administrators to retract unsatisfactory policy proposals, might very well amount to legislative veto authority. But report-and-waits raise no separation of powers problems because they assert no power to shortcut the legislative process.[55] Congressional oversight through such informal procedures might create other types of problems—undue delay in the implementation of rules, perhaps, or other infirmities of micromanagement generally. Since such problems occur within the framework of the separation of powers, however, appealing to the constitutionally mandated procedures for legislative action can do little to help solve them.

Those who hoped that upholding separation of powers procedures would undermine congressional power challenged the Supreme Court's distinction in *Chadha* between informal, legislative veto–like mechanisms and compulsory legislative vetoes. These critics of congressional power argued that informal oversight mechanisms were just as unconstitutional as legislative vetoes because both allowed members to affect policy outcomes without fulfilling all of the requirements of the legislative process.[56]

The courts considered and rejected this claim in a set of cases involving a report-and-wait provision governing activities of the General Services Administration. These cases were brought to court soon after *Chadha* declared the legislative veto unconstitutional. On first hearing, the U.S. Court of Claims struck down the report-and-wait provision as a violation of the separation of powers. It found that while the provision in the statute "may be facially inoffensive," it was evident, from "congressional and agency practice" that the provision was operating as "a *de facto* . . . congressional veto."[57]

On appeal, however, the distinction between formal and informal legislative vetoes was upheld. The Appeals Court fully recognized that report-and-wait provisions often operate exactly as legislative vetoes, noting that "committee chairmen and members naturally develop interest and expertise in the subjects entrusted to their continuing surveillance. Officials in the executive branch have to take these committees into account and keep them informed, respond to their inquiries, and it may be, flatter and please them when necessary."[58] Nonetheless, the court concluded, "there is nothing unconstitutional about this: indeed, our separation of powers makes such informal cooperation much more necessary than it would be in a pure system of parliamentary government."[59] It would be wrong to presume, in other words, that enforcement of the legislative procedures mandated by the separation of powers system would minimize Congress's role in the policymaking process.[60]

Executive branch officials who carried this faulty presumption learned the errors of their ways through political experience, which quickly taught them not to expect the Supreme Court's enforcement of separation of powers procedures to provide them with new freedom from congressional control. They learned this lesson well in the controversy over the legal status of the committee reports that usually accompany appropriations bills. These reports, which often contain specific directives on how an agency should spend money, do not have the status of law because they are not subject to approval by both chambers or to presidential veto. James Miller, Director of the Office of Management and Budget (OMB) in the Reagan administration, attempted to curtail the congressional practice of using committee reports to earmark money for particular projects by appealing to the reasoning used by the Supreme Court in invalidating the legislative veto. Appropriations committee reports are "neither voted on by Congress nor presented to the president, [so they] are not law," Miller declared in a letter sent to all federal agency heads.[61] Consequently, he announced that executive branch agencies would no longer follow the directives in committee reports.

In response to Miller's declaration, members threatened to "retaliate by tying the administration's hands with even stricter," legally binding, restrictions on spending decisions.[62] Soon thereafter, Miller sent a second letter to all federal agency heads reversing his original statement. Though Miller was on solid legal ground in pointing out that report language is not legally binding, he was politically inastute in believing that he could appeal to separation of powers procedures to preclude members from using informal controls. In conceding defeat, Miller concluded that "I believe the congressional leadership is now fully aware of the principle involved."[63] "We have made our point," his press secretary added. "We wanted to call attention to Congress and the public that report language was not legally binding."[64] This principle was not a great revelation to members of Congress. Nor did it strike them as having much political consequence.

But most executive branch officials did not need an embarrassing lesson in congressional power to realize that *Chadha* was of little practical value. This is evident from examination of the White House strategy for responding to the loss of the legislative veto, which consisted essentially of dampening enthusiasm among executive branch officials for challenging congressional oversight. White House officials in the Reagan administration knew that there were no gains to be won from *Chadha* because they were well aware that Congress's power to exercise control over administration did not depend on shortcuts through constitutional procedure.

The administration also knew that influential committee chairmen and party leaders had always opposed, albeit quietly, the enactment of legislative vetoes. Consequently, it expected them to be sympathetic to its objective of diffusing the interbranch power struggle surrounding the legislative veto issue. The administration called private meetings with powerful committee chairmen and congressional party leaders to assure them that it did not intend to test the practical value of the potential executive branch victories implied by *Chadha*. "The legislative veto was really a backbencher's idea," explained one of the White House officials, referring to members of the House who valued the symbolic power of the mechanism because they had little seniority, lacked committee or party leadership positions, and thus had few opportunities to attract attention to themselves.[65] "So even though the backbenchers would keep running around screaming and yelling and threatening us for a while, we knew that the committee chairmen would ultimately prevent them from doing anything other than letting off steam as long as we convinced them that we didn't plan to try any tricks."[66]

In addition to meeting privately with influential congressional leaders, administration officials testified publicly that they would not attempt to turn the loss of the legislative veto into an opportunity for undermining Congress's role in the policymaking process. Deputy Attorney General Edward C. Schmultz told the House Judiciary Committee: "I want to emphasize as strongly as possible that the executive branch will continue, as it has done in the past, to observe scrupulously the 'reporting' and 'waiting' features that are central to virtually all existing legislative veto devices." He concluded his testimony by assuring the committee that the administration was intent on responding to the loss of the legislative veto with a "spirit of comity and mutual respect."[67] Deputy Secretary of State Kenneth W. Dam testified, similarly, that "the *practice* of executive-legislative relations need not undergo any immediate or radical change in the wake of *Chadha* . . . [because it] does not affect other statutory procedures by which Congress is informed of or involved in actions by the Executive Branch."[68]

Another part of the Reagan administration's strategy for diffusing the legislative veto controversy was to accept that statutes containing veto provisions would remain unamended. Technically, the Justice Department could have called upon all executive branch agencies to cease complying with any of these "tainted" statutes. But as a participant in the White House policy council that developed the strategy for dealing with the legislative veto controversy explained:

> We decided not to ask the Hill to repeal all of those provisions that were clearly unconstitutional because it would just be an unnecessary workload for them. It was already clear that we had nothing to gain from trying to find ways of using *Chadha* to alter interbranch relations under any of these statutes, so we just agreed that those tainted legislative vetoes were no longer operable but that the rest of the statute remained unaffected.[69]

Finally, the White House sent a memo to the heads of all executive departments directing them to "avoid unnecessary confrontation with the Legislative branch" over the legislative veto issue.[70] Though individual bureaucrats might have expressed enthusiasm for the potential executive branch victories implied by Congress's loss of legislative veto power, administration policy on this matter reflected a clear understanding that any attempt to exercise a newfound aggressiveness would simply give Congress an excuse to use any of its many powers to lash back at executive power.

Though clearly mistaken, imprecise definitions of "legislative veto" continue to feed the widespread claim that Congress has failed to comply with the Supreme Court's invalidation of the mechanism. Thus, when Secretary of State James Baker and congressional leaders announced, in March 1989, a "gentleman's agreement" that conditioned continued aid to the Nicaraguan Contras on congressional approval, the agreement became the focus of a so-called "legislative veto" controversy that flared on the front pages of newspapers.[71] Though the agreement was perfectly constitutional—it imposed no legal obligation on the president's authority to extend Contra aid—C. Boyden Gray, President Bush's White House counsel, publicly attacked Baker for enabling congressional leaders to resurrect the unconstitutional legislative veto mechanism.[72] Analysts concluded that "the legislative veto is still alive and well more than five years after its supposed demise."[73]

Claims of Congress's noncompliance are also based on the finding that some appropriations bills enacted after *Chadha* have contained unconstitutional legislative veto provisions.[74] Yet, these claims ignore the unique legal status of appropriations bills. In so doing, they mistakenly generalize from the appropriations context to the formal congressional oversight of policy implementation at issue in *Chadha*.[75]

Unlike other types of legislation, appropriations bills do not become permanent law. Because of this unique legal status, the "appropriations context is . . . one of extraordinary reliance on legislative history enforced by politics."[76] None of the staff members of any of the appropriations subcommittees claimed that the so-called "legislative veto" provisions appearing in appropriations bills had the force of law—"but that's okay," one of the staffers explained, paraphrasing many of his colleagues,

> because they hold up in the court of common sense very nicely. We don't need any special oversight tools to make sure that agencies come back to us to get prior approval before they shift funds around inside an account. This prior approval procedure comes from very long-established informal agreements about how agencies can spend their monies. And it's rare when they show up in the law anyway. They're usually in report language.[77]

The tripartite constitutional structure obviously does not demand that members of Congress refrain from overseeing executive affairs. Those who insist on claiming otherwise might succeed in furthering some particular partisan interest; but they mischaracterize the extent to which the separation of powers structure can prevent members from participating in the implementation of policy.

The Legislative Veto's Policymaking Power

The legislative veto mechanism that was indeed struck down as a violation of the separation of powers was valuable essentially as a symbol of congressional resurgence rather than as an instrument for determining policy outcomes. This is evident from a brief review of the historical context in which the legislative veto seemed like an indispensable policymaking instrument.

Legal scholars have traced earlier manifestations of the legislative veto back to the very first session of Congress in 1789, but the veto mechanism that explicitly shortcut constitutional procedure developed in the 1930s, "in response to the problems of reorganizing the sprawling government structure created in response to the Depression."[78] The mechanism was less important in political practice than in academic circles until the 1970s, when it began to be touted as a necessary congressional control tool.[79] The reasons for this are twofold. One involves the resurgence of Congress against what had become an "Imperial" postwar presidency. The other involves congressional attempts to gain control over the "new regulatory regime" that grew out of the social regulation and regulatory reforms of the 1960s and 1970s.[80]

The Congress that was preparing to enter the decade of the 1970s was much different from the one that prompted Woodrow Wilson to call for constitutional reform at the turn of the century. Wilson complained that over the course of the Constitution's first century, Congress "entered more and more into the details of administration until it has virtually taken into its own hands all the substantial powers of government."[81] Indeed, throughout the nineteenth century, Congress was generally the dominant branch. But the political forces and demands that arose at the turn of the century led to a change in the interbranch balance of power. In particular, tremendous economic growth and the emergence of the United States as a world power created a need for executive power unfettered by detailed legislative control. Soon after these developments began to result in the expansion of executive power, the government's response to the Great Depression and to World War II delivered "the *coup de grace* to legislative supremacy."[82]

In the postwar period, bipartisanship in foreign policy helped sustain presidential dominance. The Cold War policy of containment of communism, in a period overshadowed by the threat of nuclear war, carried with it the presumption that unchecked executive power was necessary for national security. The consequences of New Deal domestic policies also served to uphold executive branch dominance in the postwar period. The creation of large-scale social service agencies during the Roosevelt administration led a majority of American citizens to expect tangible benefits from government agencies. As a result, interest groups began to lobby Congress to delegate more of its policymaking authorities to these agencies.[83]

The early 1970s brought a commitment to assertiveness among members who no longer wanted Congress to be perceived as weak and subservient. Awash in Vietnam and Watergate, the nation was becoming increasingly wary of the "Imperial Presidency," and looked to Congress to control the exercise of government power. As the Watergate scandal unfolded, constituents were eager to see their representatives engage in activities that seemed to tighten controls on executive branch discretion.[84] Nixon further fanned the flames of suspicion toward executive power by directing agencies to thwart the policies enacted by a Democrat-controlled Congress. As a result, Congress could no longer "safely assume that Presidential power would be used benignly or prudently."[85]

In the context of this drive to reassert congressional over executive power, the legislative veto acquired widespread popularity among members of Congress. The exponential growth in the number of legislative veto provisions enacted in the early 1970s reflected its apparent capacity to serve as a solution not only to the problem of the "Imperial Presidency," but also to the need for new controls over regulatory authority. In fact, "Congress passed more regulatory statutes" between 1968 and 1978 "than it had in the nation's previous 179 years."[86] In the late 1960s, the *Federal Register* averaged 20,000 pages per year. In 1971, the figure had risen to 25,442; by 1973 to 35,586; and by 1980 it exceeded 60,000 pages.[87] The delegation of regulatory authority to independent or executive agencies had always been accompanied by worries about protecting Congress's pride of place in the lawmaking process. The innovative veto mechanism promised to allow Congress to "regain" some of the power it had "lost to administrative agencies during the twentieth century."[88] To garner support for the mechanism, Rep. Elliott Levitas, the legislative veto's greatest advocate, asked his colleagues to consider: "Who makes the laws in this country—the elected Representatives of the people or the unelected bureaucrats?"[89]

But the legislative veto was only one of many procedural innovations, naturally, inspired by the congressional need for enhanced control. "When Congress delegates but does not trust," after all, "it reaches for any means at its disposal to ensure that governmental power is not misused."[90] Those who failed to take this into account suffered from the "commonly" held misconception that the legislative veto was a creative new substitute for weaker, existing legislative controls.[91] The reason for this misconception was that the legislative veto was the only control mechanism in Congress's large bag of resurgent tricks that went so far as to amend constitutional procedure. The legislative veto attracted undue attention as a policymaking instrument because of its constitutionally suspect status. Such status gave it unique power to announce the great lengths to which members were willing to go in order to address the grave problems facing the nation.

The great success of the legislative veto as a symbol of congressional control over administration is precisely what led a minority of members to oppose it. Because it was much less relevant to members' demands for control over actual policy outcomes than it was to symbolizing congressional power, opponents of the legislative veto worried that it would, paradoxically, undermine congressional oversight. Senator Wendell Ford (D-KY), for example, complained that the legislative veto "is just a piece of legislation to go back home to our business people and beat our chests and say, 'Look what we have done. We have suppressed those regulatory agencies because we are going to look at the rules.'. . . The legislative veto, in my opinion, is being used as a substitute for congressional direction and policy guidance to agencies. We are abdicating the responsibility our constituencies expect of us."[92] The veto's popularity was a problem for Senator Ford precisely because it "provides only for an up or down vote on [particular] rules and does not provide a substitute for regular and periodic oversight. . . . [It] give[s] the false—and I underscore 'false impression'—that the agencies are under control, and that no more congressional oversight is necessary. In my opinion that is hogwash."[93]

Recent studies of congressional oversight confirm that the legislative veto never functioned as a significant mechanism for affecting policy outcomes. In the most extensive study of congressional oversight mechanisms to date, Joel Aberbach found that of the fourteen oversight techniques examined in his study of the 95th Congress (1977–78), the legislative veto ranked fourteenth in frequency of use.[94] And of the fourteen techniques, he found that the legislative veto ranked ninth in effectiveness. "For proponents of the legislative veto," Aberbach concludes, "this is probably a disappointing figure since it indicates that even users do not tend to rate the veto at the top of the effectiveness scale."[95]

By rolling up his sleeves and immersing himself in the actual workings of congressional oversight, Aberbach saw clearly the distinction between the formal legislative veto declared unconstitutional by the Supreme Court and the informal legislative veto that operates under report-and-wait provisions. "A possible reason for the veto not receiving a higher effectiveness score," he suggests, "is that 'non-statutory substitutes' for the veto seem to work equally well."[96] Procedures that were not technically legislative vetoes, in other words, were the ones that actually did serve members in their quest to exercise control over the policymaking process.

The main force behind the growth of the legislative veto's symbolic power was freshman member of Congress Elliott Levitas. Having grabbed onto the legislative veto as a tool that could at once make him popular at home and give him a mark of distinction within Congress, Levitas took it upon himself in the 1970s to try to convince his colleagues that legislative veto authority was an essential and legitimate congressional prerogative. One member later commented: "Levitas quickly became a royal pain in the neck about his legislative veto pet. He got amendments added in committee or on the floor to countless pieces of legislation—anything with regulatory power included— which of course in this day and age means practically every piece of legislation outside of appropriations bills. We were constantly fighting him off."[97]

A testament to Levitas's success is that the Congress of the 1970s behaved like "a field of flowers, bending inexorably toward the sunlight of a hot new idea that promises to make all pain and complications go away."[98] This success, explained one former staff member of the House Subcommittee on Administrative Law, was due to the fact that the legislative veto "was a great tool that members could use as show-and-tell in their districts to say they were beating up on pointy-headed bureaucrats."[99] This symbolic power made it possible for Levitas to get boilerplate legislative veto provisions enacted into statutes somewhat routinely, without much attention to whether they could actually ever prove useful to members in the implementation of the statute in question.

An example of the consequences of Levitas's "single-minded determination" to enact as many legislative veto provisions as possible helps clarify why so many unconstitutional provisions have remained unamended.[100] It also illuminates why those that have been amended represent little more than congressional housecleaning. The legislative veto in the Federal Insecticide, Fungicide and Rodenticide Act (FIFRA) was not enacted until 1980 even though Levitas had tried to insert veto provisions in previous FIFRA reauthorizations.[101] A previous attempt had failed in 1978 because the veto was considered unnecessary and superfluous.[102] In response to Levitas's asking why his attempt to include a legislative veto had been prevented by the conference committee, Rep. Thomas Foley (D-WA) explained that "the Act [already] contains highly elaborate prospective review provisions before any action can be adopted."[103] In addition, Foley noted, since "this committee has followed the practice of keeping the program under such short authorization so that the entire program is subject to frequent review, we felt that the specific regulation review by both Houses of Congress would not be necessary."[104] When the same arguments for and against the veto were made again in the subsequent reauthorization cycle, however, Levitas got his way by virtue of his annoying persistence. The veto remained as unnecessary in 1980 as it had been in 1978. But it also remained as much of a valuable "credit-claimer" for members intent on acknowledging their constituents' skepticism about government regulation.[105]

The unconstitutional provision remained unamended until 1988, when the reauthorization of FIFRA gave Congress the opportunity to clean out obsolete provisions. The legislative veto was then amended to a report-and-wait provision.[106] When asked if this amendment had changed the balance of power between the branches in this particular statute, relevant government officials, industry representatives, and congressional staff all found different reasons to say "no." An attorney in the legal counsel's office at the Environmental Protection Agency (EPA) noted that "*Chadha* didn't make report-and-waits unconstitutional. And that is where Congress's power is—keeping the administrative burden on us to report all of our regulations up there."[107] One of the directors of a pesticide lobby group explained that the elimination of the legislative veto made no practical difference because it had never been valued as a way of controlling EPA's pesticide licensing activities:

> The FIFRA legislative veto was a two-chamber veto. So to use it, we would have had to have the committee bring our concerns onto the floor. That is not something we ever wanted to do. It was much easier for us to work our concerns solely through the committee and the agency. Now, you don't need to interpret this in a sinister way. It's not that we wanted to keep things off the floor because we were making off like bandits somewhere. It's just that the issues involved in these licenses are very technical. And bringing these issues onto the floor would have risked touching irrelevant political hot potatoes.[108]

One congressional staff member who had worked on the FIFRA statute since the enactment of the legislative veto echoed these explanations of the mechanism's insignificance. "They put the legislative veto in there," she said, "because it was a very popular way to show that they were doing something about controlling the growth of government. There was a big perceived need for having a legislative veto but it never really did that much for us in terms of controlling the agency, so when *Chadha* turned it into a report-and-wait, nothing changed."[109] Acknowledging that the legislative veto was a powerful symbol of congressional control is a far cry, evidently, from establishing the mechanism's indispensability to the policymaking process.

THE LEGISLATIVE VETO ON THE BOOKS

Many scholars and commentators nevertheless fail to make the distinction between the symbolic power of the veto mechanism and its actual role in the policymaking process. Thus, the surprisingly large number of legislative veto provisions that remain on the books unamended is adduced as evidence that the mechanism was playing too important a role in the policymaking process for Congress to comply with *Chadha*.[110]

But the legislative veto did not acquire popularity among members because of any proven capacity to increase congressional control over policy outcomes. Members enacted it into large numbers of statutes in the 1970s because they valued its power to symbolize congressional prerogatives. It is no surprise, therefore, that so many legislative veto provisions remain unamended today because most of them became moot, for all policymaking intents and purposes, as in the case of the FIFRA veto provision, as soon as they were enacted into law. These unamended veto provisions, explained one staffer on the House Merchant Marine Committee, are "sort of like garbage in the corner of your room. If it doesn't bother you, you don't know it's there. If it gets in your way, then you'll clean it up."[111]

Contrary to what many legislative veto analysts seem to have presumed, a situation in which federal statutes contain provisions that are "obsolete yet unrepealed . . . is neither unprecedented nor unconstitutional."[112] The situation is so common, in fact, that one prominent legal scholar argues that the courts should be made responsible for discarding obsolete provisions even when these provisions raise no constitutional problems. Otherwise, federal statute books will be inconsistent with the legal dynamics of society because inertia makes Congress incapable of repealing obsolete statutes.[113]

This rather extreme argument calls upon the courts to organize the messy statutes produced by Congress's decentralized and institutionally fragmented legislative process. It assumes that all new statutes should be woven into the existing statutory framework in a consistent and logical manner, and that every statute that remains on the books should continue to operate as originally intended. But, in fact, "nothing in democratic theory requires that legislatures should act in a sober or considered manner."[114] This is particularly important for students of American politics to appreciate because, in comparison to parliamentary systems, the American political system is noteworthy for endowing its national legislature with the authority to enact into law provisions that are not relevant to the policy issues at hand.[115]

By assuming that the veto mechanism was functionally significant simply because it was frequently enacted into law, the conventional wisdom reveals that it rests on an apolitical understanding of the legislative process.[116] If the practical value of the veto shortcut as a congressional control tool was indeed guaranteed by mere enactment, then certainly the separation of powers system, which prohibits such enactment, would be responsible for hindering Congress's capacity to participate in the policymaking process. Such would be the logical conclusion from a Wilsonian perspective, a perspective that evaluates the American political system simply by examining the profusion of procedural restraints imposed on policymaking by the Constitution.

But empirical evidence reveals that the legislative veto shortcut authority was superfluous to the informal interbranch contacts and negotiations that serve as the real workhorse of congressional oversight power. At the very least, then, exposing the myth of the legislative veto shows that American government has much more play in its structural joints than the Wilsonian critique of the separation of powers can account for.[117]

Chapter Four

THE LEGISLATIVE VETO OVER THE FEDERAL TRADE COMMISSION

Most telling of the legislative veto's potential to alter the balance of policymaking power between the branches was the widespread popularity of generic legislative veto bills. These bills, which began to be introduced in the mid-1970s, would have granted Congress legislative veto authority over any regulation issued by an independent agency or executive branch department, thereby making it unnecessary to enact statute-by-statute veto provisions. The proponents of the generic veto bills attracted supporters by complaining that agencies possessed excessive rulemaking authority. They claimed that "structural change" in the separation of powers system was the only answer to "this serious and growing problem." Only with the authority to shortcut the constitutionally mandated restrictions on the use of legislative power could Congress begin to reassert its much-needed authority and control over the regulatory process.[1]

Congress never enacted a generic veto bill. But generic veto bill advocates claimed a partial victory when they succeeded in enacting a legislative veto provision into the Federal Trade Commission (FTC) statute. More than any other agency, the FTC used its regulatory powers in ways that exemplified the problems that generic veto bill advocates hoped to solve. Even in the case of the FTC veto, however, empirical examination reveals that the legislative veto was ill suited to enhance congressional control over delegated authorities. More importantly, it shows how the constitutional system of separated powers forced a profound restructuring, by the early 1980s, of regulatory authorities and policies that had fueled demands for a generic legislative veto.

THE IMPORTANCE OF THE FTC LEGISLATIVE VETO

The FTC of the 1970s provided generic veto bill advocates with powerful evidence for their claim that regulatory agencies were out of control. One such advocate, Rep. Robert E. Bauman (R-MD), testified that "although instances of overregulation are endless, the prime example of an agency gone mad is the Federal Trade Commission."[2] Similarly, Rep. Ted Risenhoover (D-OK) exclaimed that "of all the agencies which are running amok, the Federal Trade Commission is the absolute worst example."[3] Above all, Rep. Elliott Levitas (D-GA), the most outspoken of those members who claimed that Congress needed to grant itself generic legislative veto authority spanning independent and executive branch regulatory agencies, singled out the FTC as the agency most representative of the need for new tools of congressional oversight. The FTC's status as an independent agency allowed it to become, in Levitas's eyes, the most egregious offender against the values of democratic accountability. "I wonder how many people in the United States know the names of, much less have the opportunity of voting for, the five commissioners of the FTC. Yet," Levitas exclaimed, "the FTC can pass legislation, if you will, of real legislative policy, without any accountability to anybody."[4]

The FTC was of particular concern to generic veto advocates because its statutory authority was extremely broad. In expanding the FTC's regulatory powers in the Magnuson-Moss Warranty–Federal Trade Commission Improvement Act in 1975, Congress enacted "the most far-reaching expansion of FTC power to affect marketers since the FTC Act was passed in 1914."[5] Magnuson-Moss explicitly granted the FTC the power to promulgate rules that would have "the force and effect of law."[6] This power to promulgate rules included, explicitly, rules meant to prohibit "unfair or deceptive" practices.[7] Without any statutory guidance as to what an "unfair" practice might be, however, the Magnuson-Moss delegation of rulemaking authority to the FTC was seen by those who called for a generic legislative veto as unjustifiably unlimited. They viewed such broad delegation as "altogether outside the mainstream of our constitutional tradition" because it allowed for "an aggregation of powers in a government agency not directly responsible to voters or to elected officials."[8]

The FTC became subject to a torrent of criticism from critics of overregulation as soon as it began to take advantage of its newly sanctioned authority. Soon after the enactment of Magnuson-Moss, the Bureau of Consumer Protection within the agency initiated eighteen major consumer protection rulemakings addressing alleged anticonsumer activity.[9] Industry groups perceived these new rulemakings as tinged with the spirit of "zealotry and inquisition," and so viewed with alarm the proposed regulation of many business practices and industries that had never before been subject to federal regulation.[10] In response to the FTC's early attempts to make full use of its Magnuson-Moss authorities, those business interests that stood to be affected by the FTC's proposed rules—"doctors, lawyers, funeral home directors, auto manufacturers and used car dealers, advertisers of all shapes and sizes, big oil, the cereal industry"—together with those who feared they would be next on the FTC's hit list, began to complain about the agency's extensive powers.[11] Since small industries were the ones most directly affected by the agency's proposed rulemakings, the FTC "managed to alienate the leading citizens of every town and city."[12] As a result, "there wasn't a member of Congress that hadn't been bitched to about the FTC."[13]

The image of the FTC as "a rogue agency run amok" was intimately tied to members' support for the legislative veto mechanism.[14] Levitas's 1976 version of a generic legislative veto bill would not have come as close to passing as it did had it not been for the enactment of Magnuson-Moss in 1975. Many members chose to support Levitas's generic veto bill, in other words, because they feared the aggrandizement of FTC power created by Magnuson-Moss.[15] Though their continued attempts to pass a generic legislative veto bill in the 1980s were unsuccessful, proponents of these bills claimed a significant victory in Congress's enactment of a legislative veto into the FTC Reauthorization Act in 1980.[16] For Levitas, the 1980 FTC legislative veto, a two-house disapproval resolution procedure, was a "success of particular satisfaction."[17]

At the same time that the FTC veto represented the most important victory of those pushing the generic veto cause, it also represented, naturally, a unique new restriction on the powers of the agency itself. It was warmly received as a new weapon by those intent on bringing the FTC under tighter congressional control. Some members considered it so indispensable to have legislative veto authority over FTC rulemaking, in fact, that they successfully threatened to cut off all further funding for the commission unless its reauthorization legislation in the late 1970s contained a veto provision.[18] Even though President Carter had vehemently opposed the legislative veto provision during most of the reauthorization process, he ultimately accepted it as the price for allowing the FTC to remain in operation.[19] When the Supreme Court invalidated all legislative vetoes in *Chadha*, FTC-watchers feared that the commission "could once again become the run-away agency [Congress] had succeeded in curbing through the veto."[20] They believed the legislative veto to have been distinctly necessary for pulling in the reins on the FTC, an agency that had acted as if its mission was "to boldly regulate where no Federal agency has ever regulated before."[21]

Advocates of the FTC veto quickly learned that they had little to fear from the Supreme Court's invalidation of the mechanism. The commission's reputation as a "bully," a "National Nanny," and "an agency largely out of control" quickly lost its currency in the 1980s.[22] In stark contrast to its reputation during the 1970s, the FTC during the 1980s was diagnosed as having "a near fatal case of the 'slows'— never have so many labored so energetically to produce so little."[23] The agency practically ceased enforcing its own rules in the 1980s, and it did not propose any new rules.[24] The Supreme Court's elimination of the legislative veto could not have much of an affect on policy outcomes, obviously, because there was little policy coming out of the agency that would have been subject to the legislative veto if the Supreme Court had upheld the veto's constitutionality. Designed to curb an FTC that "bit off more than it could chew," the legislative veto issue became moot in the 1980s as the FTC became an agency that was "suffering from anorexia nervosa."[25]

The arrival of the Reagan administration in 1981 brought with it a "concerted and far-reaching commitment to reduce government intervention in the American economy."[26] It dramatically minimized the volume of FTC consumer protection rulemaking partly by appointing officials to the agency who claimed with pride that they "tried to do everything President Reagan would want . . . and less."[27] The administration also slashed the FTC's budget, thereby making it difficult for the agency to fulfill its responsibilities as an enforcement agency, let alone as an agency supposedly eager to produce industry-wide regulations.[28]

In reversing the ideological convictions governing the FTC's activities, the Reagan administration had direct support from the agency's congressional oversight committees. Though these committees had encouraged the FTC's regulatory activism in the early 1970s, by the late 1970s they had turned to attacking the agency's ambitious rulemaking ventures.[29] During most of the 1970s, these committees were filled with members who supported the consumer movement's activist regulatory policies.[30] But in the late 1970s, they underwent a turnover in membership that forced the beginning of a drastic reversal in FTC activism.[31]

Changes in the political climate affecting regulatory policy seem to provide a self-evident explanation for why the Supreme Court's invalidation of the legislative veto had little impact on the FTC. Yet, an examination of the sources and consequences of the FTC's controversial regulatory activities in the 1970s reveals that the FTC veto would have remained inconsequential to policy outcomes even if the Supreme Court had upheld its constitutionality, and if the Reagan administration had been followed by elected officials intent on reviving the activist regulatory policies of the 1970s.

THE WORKINGS OF THE FTC VETO

To explain why the FTC veto never did, nor ever would have played a significant role in the policymaking process, this study analyzes three related empirical observations. First, a close look at the rulemakings responsible for the agency's "runaway" reputation reveals that the legislative veto could never have served congressional needs to rein in the agency. Secondly, a study of the ways in which the mechanism did serve congressional needs demonstrates that these needs were essentially symbolic, and thus not tied to any particular policy objectives. Finally, a solid understanding of the FTC's controversial policies of the 1970s, and of the political forces that made the legislative veto popular as an antidote to these policies, shows that the veto lost its popularity and would have been unlikely to ever become popular again, irrespective of the Supreme Court's invalidation of the mechanism or of the ideological changes of the 1980s.

THE FEDERAL TRADE COMMISSION

The Legislative Veto and Congressional Control Needs

Tracing the evolution of the FTC's rulemaking authority shows why the FTC veto never became and could never become a significant instrument of congressional control. Prior to the adoption of Magnuson-Moss in 1975, the FTC did not possess explicit authority to promulgate industry-wide rules to regulate business practices. The controversy surrounding the agency's first attempt to promulgate such a rule, a trade regulation rule governing cigarette advertising that was proposed in 1963, was mooted when Congress implemented the FTC's proposed rule by statute.[32] The next major rulemaking effort came in 1971, when the FTC issued a rule that required octane ratings to be posted on gasoline pumps. The rule was immediately taken to court and struck down by the District of Columbia District Court. When the Court of Appeals reversed this decision, the FTC received, for the first time, judicial recognition of its asserted rulemaking authority.[33]

At about the same time as the ambiguities surrounding the FTC's rulemaking authority landed in court, the agency came under a barrage of attacks for lacking direction, being poorly managed, being "obsessed with trivia and woefully inefficient."[34] These attacks were launched through reports on the FTC released by Ralph Nader in January 1969 and by the American Bar Association, at the request of President Nixon, in September 1969.[35] In addition, consumer protection activists became committed, in the 1970s, to confirming the authority of the FTC to "promulgate substantive trade regulation rules— to legislate before the fact instead of having to proceed case-by-case against individual businesses."[36] Faced with demands to grant the FTC rulemaking authority, members themselves began to debate "the existence and wisdom" of such authority.[37] The Court of Appeals legitimized the FTC's rulemaking power by upholding the octane-rate rule in 1973, but the agency did not receive congressional confirmation of its rulemaking authority until 1975, when Congress enacted Magnuson-Moss.[38]

Partly because it had never been entirely clear to members whether the FTC had the authority to engage in rulemaking, "the legislative history of Magnuson-Moss reflect[ed] widespread congressional concern over the scope of the power delegated to the Commission."[39] This congressional concern that the FTC might become too powerful was also due to the agency's claim that it intended to use "unfairness" as a justification for rulemaking. Though the FTC based its first use of rulemaking authority in 1963 on the grounds that certain types of cigarette advertising were "unfair," it did not threaten to continue promulgating such rules until the Supreme Court "blessed" the criteria by which the cigarette rule had defined unfairness.[40] The FTC took this 1972 court case, the *S&H* case, "as a legal blessing for a wide-ranging attack on any practice that might have any adverse effect on any consumer."[41] The Supreme Court's endorsement, in *S&H,* of FTC authority to regulate against "unfair" practices, combined with the explicit delegation of rulemaking authority proposed in Magnuson-Moss, made members especially attentive to fashioning proper restrictions on FTC rulemaking. Together, these authorizations would make the FTC's power to regulate business "virtually as broad as that of the Congress itself."[42]

Members' solution to their concern for the great rulemaking discretion lodged in the FTC was to impose special procedural requirements on the agency. Magnuson-Moss thus consisted of procedures for promulgating rules that were much more elaborate than the generic Administrative Procedure Act (APA) notice-and-comment procedures, which require all agencies to publish proposed rules in the *Federal Register,* and to invite comments from interested parties, before promulgating proposed rules as final rules.[43] In addition, Magnuson-Moss imposed "hybrid rulemaking" procedures on the FTC, which required the agency to hold actual hearings on its proposed rules and to allow for cross-examination of witnesses at these hearings. Members valued this hybrid rulemaking process because it greatly enhanced participatory rights for interested parties.[44] By forcing the FTC to develop rules in very close contact with the public, members intended to restrict the breadth of discretionary authority lodged in the agency.[45]

As the principal restraint placed on the broad rulemaking authority delegated to the FTC in Magnuson-Moss, the hybrid rulemaking procedure quickly proved to be insufficient. It did not prevent the FTC from engaging in rulemakings that led members to believe that the agency was exceeding its authority. The entire seven-day, eight-hundred-page set of oversight hearings on the FTC in 1979, in fact, resulted from the failure of hybrid rulemaking procedures to restrain the agency's exercise of its authorities. "Throughout these hearings," Senator Harrison H. Schmitt (R-NM) noted at the time, "we've heard time and time again that the FTC has exceeded its authority. We have heard time and time again that the FTC is prepared to impose a bracket of regulations over commercial activities that are currently either not regulated at all, or which are regulated by the States."[46] Thus, in spite of the elaborate hybrid rulemaking procedures built into Magnuson-Moss as safeguards against improper uses of the rulemaking authority, members of Congress and many groups within the private sector developed strong objections to the FTC's rulemaking activities of the mid-1970s.[47]

Indeed, understanding the particular way in which the hybrid rulemaking procedures proved to be a failure illuminates the key mistake of the FTC's regulatory policy in the 1970s. The complaints and criticisms of those who viewed the FTC as a runaway agency were not directed at the agency's promulgation of final rules (i.e., those actually decided upon), but at the way in which the agency proposed new rules and managed the intermediate stages of rulemaking.[48] The main problem did not lie in the rules that the FTC was actually implementing. It rested in the agency's seeming inability to "restrain its staff and itself from initiating costly and highly questionable investigations . . . [in areas] where no demonstrated prevalence of such unfair and deceptive acts and practices [was] in evidence."[49] The virulent objections associated with the FTC as a runaway were directed at the agency's practically unlimited discretion to *initiate* rulemaking proceedings.

The hybrid rulemaking procedures made it impossible for the FTC to develop industry-wide rules away from public scrutiny. Hybrids did not, however, create any statutory standards for determining whether the agency was justified in initiating a rulemaking investigation against a particular industry. Consequently, "the initial documents, notices, rule provisions, and staff reports in most rulemaking proceedings [were] vague, . . . rarely delineat[ing] what the FTC was doing and why."[50] In its attempts to justify these proposed rulemakings, furthermore, the agency provided little more than anecdotal evidence. This exacerbated the controversies surrounding FTC rulemaking, one scholar of the regulatory process and former official of the FTC's Bureau of Competition explained, because

> most industries involve millions upon millions of transactions. Anecdotes regarding such activity cannot reveal whether the problem is isolated or systemic. Nor can anecdotes reveal the economic source of the problem or whether the proposed solution is sensible. At best, anecdotal evidence can indicate only that a practice exists and injures some consumers. It cannot demonstrate that the *rate* at which problems occur is

high enough to justify an industry-wide rule that will inevitably impose costs on innocent parties.[51]

The FTC's liberal use of anecdotal evidence, combined with its absolute discretion to begin proceedings for new trade regulation rules, was bound to provoke bitter objections from a wide variety of groups.

The FTC proved the hybrid procedures to be insufficient restraints on agency discretion as soon as it acquired its new powers in Magnuson-Moss. Even Michael Pertschuk, chairman of the agency during its most activist years in the 1970s and the most outspoken advocate of industry-wide rulemaking, admitted in congressional testimony in the late 1970s that "there is no question that there are occasions in the past, especially in the early rulemaking proceedings . . . in which your criticism of [FTC] staff in effect conducting a vendetta against the industries involved—there was some justice in those accusations."[52] A study of FTC rulemaking conducted by the Administrative Conference confirmed that the evidence used by the agency to justify its first wave of proposed Magnuson-Moss rules "consisted of large quantities of almost random information."[53]

Though the hybrid procedures made it highly unlikely that controversial proposals would result in final, fully implemented rules, they nonetheless allowed the agency to impose costs that industry groups considered egregiously unfair. The FTC ultimately rejected the Food Advertising Rule proposed in 1975, for example, but the rulemaking process itself "took years of effort and millions of dollars both within the Commission and within the industry." The FTC initiated the rulemaking even though it "lacked evidence on how consumers interpreted much of the advertising that the rule would have regulated, on whether most of the prohibited practices injured consumers, and on whether the remedies proposed would accomplish their goals."[54] Had FTC staff attempted to collect rigorous and systematic evidence on such questions, they would have known not to initiate such a rulemaking.

Similarly, though the hybrid procedures succeeded in forcing the FTC to whittle down the scope of the Funeral Rule, they could not restrain the agency from evoking great anger from the entire funeral home industry. Chairman Pertschuk noted, in this regard, that "I think the early days of that funeral proceeding were unfortunate in terms of both the Commission and the industry involved. There was a sense of a vendetta against the funeral industry in those early days and a feeling on the part of the funeral industry that it was not being heard and would not be heard."[55] The failure of the hybrid procedures, from the point of view of members of Congress, was that they allowed the FTC to engage in rhetoric that proved infuriating to a large number of industries. They were also a failure, ironically, because their success at preventing the FTC from implementing unpopular rules imposed heavy costs on the industry in question as well as on the agency itself. It was very expensive, in other words, for the FTC to learn through the hybrid procedures that its proposed rules were unfeasible.

At the same time that the hybrid rulemaking requirements were proving unable to prevent the FTC from using its rulemaking authority in highly contested ways, the agency's definition of an unfair business practice began to prove almost unbounded in scope. Though the Supreme Court had sanctioned unfairness as a justifiable basis for FTC rulemakings in 1972, the agency did not begin to take advantage of this sanction until Magnuson-Moss explicitly granted it authority to promulgate industry-wide rules. Once it did so, industry groups realized that neither relevant court decisions nor existing agency procedures provided restraints on the FTC's discretion to deem a particular set of practices unfair.

It became "commonplace" among legal scholars to blame the Supreme Court's *S&H* decision for enabling the agency to "create its own law."[56] The vagueness of the FTC's unfairness doctrine allowed the agency to justify its regulations with "an extremely plastic, open-ended set of theories" about the nature of unfair business practices.[57] The FTC was free to claim, for example, that a practice was "unfair" because "it offended public policy." By endowing the FTC with such power, the *S&H* decision helped fuel the agency's excesses of the 1970s and the concomitant hostility toward the agency from industry groups and members of Congress.[58]

The worst fears of those who distrusted the FTC's authority to address alleged unfairness were realized in the agency's proposal to regulate children's advertising. This "kid-vid" rule, the "pinnacle of unfocused unfairness theories in FTC rulemaking," justified a ban on all advertising directed at children by claiming that such advertising was "immoral, unscrupulous, and unethical."[59] Critics of FTC activism cited the kid-vid rule as an example of the need for added congressional controls over the FTC's authority to initiate rulemakings. Such controls would have made it possible to prevent the agency from launching the kid-vid proceeding "until there was a showing of some reasonable basis for it."[60]

Critics of regulatory activism became increasingly enamored of the legislative veto as the FTC began to flex its powerful new Magnuson-Moss muscles, and as the hybrid procedures failed to restrain the agency from initiating poorly justified rulemaking proceedings. Even if the legislative veto had been available to members during the period immediately following passage of Magnuson-Moss, however, it would not have prevented the FTC's regulatory excesses. The legislative veto, after all, was a mechanism directed at the disapproval of *final* regulations. But the agency's excesses consisted of questionable *proposed* regulations. The legislative veto could not have prevented the FTC from "harass[ing]" private industry because it focused congressional oversight "at the end" of the rulemaking process, "instead of looking at the problems on the front end" where the "harassment" was actually occurring.[61]

The legislative veto was functionally irrelevant to solving the problem of the "runaway" FTC for two reasons. Not only was it ill-suited to preventing the agency from recklessly initiating new rulemaking proceedings, but its potential to enhance congressional control over the final outcome of these proceedings was unnecessary. Existing control tools made it virtually impossible for the FTC to implement regulations that had not been highly scrutinized and molded by members and their constituencies. The extensive participation requirements associated with the hybrid rulemaking process ultimately forced the FTC to narrow the scope of every single rule it proposed. As Chairman Pertschuk noted, "every one of the rules upon which we have taken final action or nearly final action has emerged in substantially different . . . form than proposed. . . . The rulemaking process has indeed afforded those affected by proposed rules a real opportunity to be heard on the record and more."[62]

The hybrid rulemaking process was extremely successful at preventing the FTC from carrying a particularly unpopular proposed rule to its final form. The more controversial a proposed rule, the larger would be the record of hearings and cross-examinations and submissions of evidence for and against the rule. Thus, the records associated with some of the first Magnuson-Moss proposals contained literally tens of thousands of pages. The Vocational Schools Rule record, for example, contained 111,695 pages; the Used Car Rule 71,694 pages; the Mobile Homes Rule 261,405 pages; and the Credit Practices Rule 207,921 pages.[63] Clearly, members were not in need of additional mechanisms with which to increase their control over the FTC's implementation of final rules. The legislative veto might have become a significant tool of congressional participation in the policymaking process if it had provided members with some sort of restraint over the FTC's authority to initiate rulemaking proceedings. But it could not provide such restraint, so it never became a significant control tool.[64] Its noteworthy shortcut through constitutional procedure was irrelevant to members' actual demand for increased oversight power.

The Legislative Veto's Symbolic Function

The agency's regulatory excesses of the mid-1970s—the same ones, ironically, that the legislative veto was incapable of restraining—were responsible for broadening support for the FTC veto among members of Congress. Before the FTC began to initiate ill-conceived rulemakings, members did not consider the legislative veto particularly useful or necessary.[65] But at the height of the FTC's reputation as a "runaway" bureaucracy, the legislative veto seemed an indispensable congressional control tool because of its symbolic power. Even though it could not prevent the FTC from initiating rulemakings, it could "at least telescope a very important message to the agencies involved, that Congress is going to be watching very carefully over these broad social policies that these agencies take on."[66]

Both cases in which members exercised their legislative veto authority demonstrate how the actual value of the mechanism lay in its symbolic power. Congress's first and only veto of an FTC rule occurred in 1982 when members took advantage of their legislative veto authority to overturn the agency's Used Car Rule. The proposed rule would have required used car dealers to inform customers of major known defects in cars and explain the extent of warranty coverage.[67] One of the FTC's first rulemakings begun after the passage of Magnuson-Moss, the Used Car Rule attracted widespread criticism in the mid-1970s because it was "encumbered by onerous recordkeeping requirements and other restrictions on conduct that were costly, intrusive, and of questionable value to consumers."[68] Those who claimed that the legislative veto was an indispensable congressional control

59

tool believed that Congress's successful disapproval of the Used Car Rule reflected public frustration with the extremism of consumer activists.[69] Without the mechanism, in other words, Congress would have been unable to serve the public interest.

From the perspective of consumer activists, however, Congress's disapproval of the Used Car Rule served as powerful evidence that the legislative veto mechanism was corrosive of the legislative process. Noting that "$571,626 of car dealer PAC money had gone to about 85 percent of the sponsors of the veto resolution," consumer activists argued that the veto shortcut simply made it easier for industry groups to impose restrictions on the FTC's authority to regulate business practices.[70] These critics viewed the veto mechanism as responsible for encouraging "special interests to lobby against regulations they do not like," leaving the unorganized public "unable to counter the pressure."[71]

Though the Used Car Rule veto fueled heated debates over the desirability of the veto mechanism, members would have overturned the rule irrespective of the presence of a legislative veto in the FTC statute. Students of the particular political issues surrounding the Used Car Rule have concluded that "an ordinary statute . . . almost certainly would have been forthcoming to nullify the rule if the legislative veto had not been available."[72] Or, what would have been easier, and thus more likely, is that members would have vetoed the Used Car Rule by enacting a direct prohibition against it into an existing statute in much the same way that they vetoed the FTC's attempts to regulate children's advertising.[73] The legislative veto was not responsible for the success of lobbyists representing used car salesmen, in other words, because Congress's constitutional authority to pass laws would have served them just as effectively: "Well-organized, politically effective groups do not need the legislative veto to see to it that an agency rule is reversed by Congress if it [is a rule that] imposes significant costs on them but the beneficiaries of the rule are diffuse and disorganized."[74] Had Congress overturned the Used Car Rule in an ordinary manner, it would not have received nearly as much attention as it did by shortcutting constitutional procedure. Though the veto mechanism was unnecessary for controlling policy outcomes, therefore, it was noteworthy for its power to draw attention to congressional oversight authority.

Analysis of Congress's second attempt to veto an FTC rule provides further evidence that the legislative veto served to symbolize congressional power, not alter policy outcomes. Intent on making use of Congress's legislative veto authority, Rep. Marty Russo (D-IL) succeeded in getting a resolution passed through the House that disapproved the FTC's Funeral Rule, but he failed to convince enough of his Senate colleagues to pass the same resolution. As a result, the Funeral Rule, requiring funeral directors to itemize their prices, became law, quietly, in May 1983.[75] More noteworthy than Russo's failure to actually veto the Funeral Rule, however, was his success at garnering as much support as he did for vetoing a rule that was admittedly mild.

Russo convinced many of his colleagues to support his disapproval resolution by ignoring the potential costs and benefits of the Funeral Rule itself. He characterized his resolution as a general reaction against the excessive federal regulation that was stifling small businesses.[76] Commissioner Pertschuk noted and complained about the symbolic power of Russo's veto resolution by explaining that Russo could "make respectable to liberals and conservatives alike his otherwise unfathomable assault on the FTC's funeral-cost disclosure rule with the following moving rhetoric: 'overregulation is already enough of a problem in the nation. Productivity is being harmed . . .' It is a little difficult to grasp the concept of productivity in funeral production."[77] Simply by voting for Russo's resolution, then, members could show that they opposed burdensome regulations.

Its formidable symbolic power notwithstanding, Russo's proposed veto of the Funeral Rule had no policy impact. Acknowledging the surprising popularity of Russo's resolution, one of the FTC officials who worked on the Funeral Rule in the Bureau of Consumer Protection explained why the veto resolution was irrelevant to the policymaking process:

> We knew, of course, that Marty Russo would introduce a disapproval resolution threatening to kill the Funeral Rule. But we went ahead with making it final anyway because we had already watered down the reg from its earlier incarnations when it had really been controversial. All that watering down, incidentally, occurred before Congress put a legislative veto in our statute. So the legislative veto didn't make much of a difference in the drafting of regs or how the reg looked in the end, but it certainly created a lot of noise.[78]

Clearly, those who claim that Congress needed the legislative veto shortcut to retain some control over FTC policymaking completely misunderstand the actual role played by the veto mechanism. As the FTC took full advantage of its broad new rulemaking powers in the mid-1970s, the legislative veto became a powerful symbol of Congress's intent to cut back on overactive regulatory agencies. But this function of the legislative veto was short-lived, for statutory, administrative, and jurisprudential changes in the late 1970s and early 1980s made moot the legislative veto's capacity to symbolize congressional oversight power.

The Legislative Veto Becomes Unnecessary

The legislative veto lost its symbolic power as the FTC ceased to initiate controversial rulemakings. The Reagan administration's crusade against regulatory activism naturally made it extremely difficult for the FTC to continue such activities.[79] Yet, the restrictions imposed on the FTC's regulatory authority in the 1980s did not result solely from the sharp ideological changes marked by the arrival of the Reagan administration. They also consisted of extensions of policies that were put in place by Congress, the courts, and the FTC itself in the late 1970s. These policies represented a direct response to the unseemly regulatory excesses that were themselves responsible for turning the legislative veto into a popular oversight mechanism. These institutional responses ensured that, irrespective of the Supreme Court's invalidation of the legislative veto, or of changes in regulatory policy brought by the Reagan administration, the symbolic power of the veto mechanism would run out of steam in the 1980s.

Even the most activist of the FTC staff believed, in retrospect, that criticisms of the agency's regulatory activism were well-grounded. By 1979 Chairman Pertschuk testified that "we've learned much from . . . criticism and from the concern raised by those, industry and consumer alike, who have participated in our rulemaking process."[80] He admitted that "Commission critics and Members of this committee have made a valid point that the proposal of broad, far-reaching rule[s], even if ultimately trimmed back by the Commission, entails substantial costs for those industries participating in the rulemaking process, and perhaps generates needless enmity."[81] Though regulatory enthusiasts at first viewed the Magnuson-Moss rulemaking authority as "a new toy," as "a piece of candy [that] seemed to be a broad panacea for many problems," experience with this new toy quickly taught the consumer protection community that "rulemaking is expensive, time-consuming and not the answer to every wrong."[82] By the late 1970s, the consensus among FTC staff was that the period immediately following passage of Magnuson-Moss was a "period of trial and error; mistakes were made."[83]

The extensive public participation requirements of the hybrid procedures played a central role in teaching FTC staff the errors of their ways. One FTC official who participated in the initial Magnuson-Moss rulemakings explained that "the hybrid rulemaking requirements encouraged groups to complain and slow down the rulemaking process even if they had very little to complain about. With the shaky evidence we used in that first set of rulemakings, there was no way we were going to get anything done. So we started to make the tightening-up of evidence standards a priority issue in the late 1970s."[84] These widely voiced complaints led Pertschuk and his staff to take "a hard look" at the agency's "pre-rulemaking proposal process."[85] As a result of this "hard look," the agency announced that it would give advance notice of, and ask for public comment on, any future intention to initiate a rulemaking.[86] Congress later enacted this advance notice procedure into law in the 1980 FTC Reauthorization.

The FTC's soul-searching "hard look" also led it to impose restrictions on its threateningly broad discretion to regulate "unfair" business practices.[87] It "expressly disavowed the notion that a practice could be unfair merely because the Commission believed it was 'immoral, unscrupulous, unethical.'"[88] Consequently, "offending public policy" would no longer be good enough reason to find a particular practice "unfair."[89]

The FTC's commitment to reforming its reckless ways in the late 1970s also led it to make greater use of its authority to "petition district courts for preliminary injunctions."[90] One of the FTC lawyers who had worked on expanding the scope of this authority, explicitly granted to the agency in §13(b) of the FTC Act, explained that

> one of the reasons that Magnuson-Moss was such a big deal is that it gave the FTC authority to demand consumer redress. By authorizing the FTC to promulgate industry-wide rules and attaching specific civil penalties to the violation of such rules, Magnuson-Moss allowed the FTC to get consumer redress for people by going into federal court whenever some business would violate one of its rules. Now, see, §13(b) allowed the FTC to go directly into court without having to point to any violated rules. Thing is, we didn't really figure out that §13(b) could be such a powerhouse until 1979 or so, when we started poking around for ways of getting things done without having to do rulemakings.[91]

The FTC's §13(b) authority to petition courts for injunctions became central to the agency's consumer protection activities as soon as the courts began handing down decisions, in 1982, favorable to the agency's desire to use the authority broadly.[92] Case-by-case demands for consumer redress were not nearly as glamorous as promulgating industry-wide rules governing business practices. But they were, and remain, politically feasible, and thus, practically achievable.

Further compelling the FTC's retreat in response to its critics was a series of court decisions that forced the agency to refrain from reckless rulemaking. These decisions did not occur until several years after the enactment of Magnuson-Moss because it took several years for the rules initiated by the FTC to reach the end of the rulemaking process. Only upon presenting final drafts of its proposed rules could the FTC be sued by "any interested person" intent on restraining the agency's regulatory powers.[93] As soon as it did so, the FTC found itself pleading guilty in courts of law as well as courts of public opinion. In both of the cases of Magnuson-Moss rules that came up for review, the court remanded the rules to the FTC, requiring the agency to narrow their scope before implementing them.[94]

The court invalidated the FTC's proposed rules because it objected to the evidence used by the agency to claim that regulation was necessary. The first time it remanded one of the FTC's rules, the court justified its objections by referring to the legislative history of Magnuson-Moss, which stated unambiguously that no FTC rule should "receive judicial approval 'unless the Commission's action was supported by substantial evidence in the record taken as a whole.'"[95] The second time an FTC rule came up for review, the court again criticized the agency's use of evidence. In reviewing the Eyeglass Rule, the court noted that while there might have been solid evidence supporting the need for regulation of optometrists when the rule was initiated in 1975, the ensuing five-year period necessary for completing the rulemaking process had seen a change in circumstances and a concomitant "diminished need for the rule."[96] As a result, the court operated according to a doctrine "favoring remand, in the interest of a just result, where there has been a change in circumstances subsequent to administrative decision."[97]

Several years elapsed before critics of the FTC's regulatory excesses could take advantage of the expanded scope of judicial review tied to rulemaking in Magnuson-Moss. Once they did, though, the courts proved, as had been expected at the time Magnuson-Moss was written, to have "a direct and substantial prophylactic" effect on the agency's rulemaking activities.[98] In describing how the court's review of Magnuson-Moss rules was instrumental in restraining the agency's powers, an FTC official in the Consumer Protection Division explained that

> back in the late 1970s, the court came down with *Gibbs*—the Vocational Schools Rule case—which really tightened up the evidence standards for justifying the beginning of a rulemaking. And then the court said in the *AOA* case—the Eyeglass Rule case—that "even if the evidence was there when you first started the rule, don't assume that you can just keep going with the rulemaking proceeding. You have to attend to the fact that the evidence might change over time." So it's no longer as easy after *Gibbs* and *AOA* to be flippant in initiating Magnuson-Moss rulemakings.[99]

In response to the court's objections, FTC staff developed a set of high standards by which they would assess the evidence justifying any future rulemakings. First announced in a 1982 staff memorandum attached to the rule meant to govern food advertising, these standards required that "the Commission should promulgate Trade Regulation rules only if the *evidentiary* record establishes (1) that there is a need for the proposed rule and (2) that the rule will likely remedy the problems identified in a way that the benefits of the rule exceed its costs."[100] The standards were soon reiterated and elaborated in the preamble to a subsequent rule that now carries the force of law.[101] Based explicitly on the court cases that imposed strict evidence standards on individual rulemaking proceedings, this preamble states as a matter of general FTC policy that "the record should contain a preponderance of substantial reliable evidence in support of a proposed rule before that rule is promulgated."[102]

Consumer protection activists who had tried and failed to make the FTC promulgate broad, industry-wide rules realized, in retrospect, that their objectives had been essentially doomed from the start. They were doomed, one long-time FTC official explained, because of the agency's wide jurisdiction:

> From the 1950s to the 70s, we went after the big oxes, like steel and tobacco. Big industries like that were concentrated in geographically discrete regions. But when Magnuson-Moss expanded our jurisdiction from commerce clause issues to anything 'in or affecting commerce,' then we could start going after businesses that didn't necessarily affect interstate commerce. So we started going after every small business in America: funeral directors, used cars dealers, insurance salesmen. So hundreds of congressmen got upset instead of the usual one or two members from

tobacco-producing states as used to be the case before Magnuson-Moss. At any rate, we've learned our political lesson.[103]

One consumer advocate who had served as an FTC commissioner in the mid-1970s noted, similarly, that "when you engage in rulemaking, you virtually mobilize the whole industry against you. Good rulemaking seizes on a single and narrow aspect of business activity and goes after it. Bad rulemaking regulates everything in sight. In the mid-1970s, we were doing bad rulemaking, so it's no surprise that we got pretty heavily battered."[104]

Having learned the errors of its rulemaking ways, the FTC increasingly turned to case-by-case adjudication in protecting consumer interests. "Rulemaking," one former FTC official of the Pertschuk era explained, "can have its harshest effects on the most responsible companies in an industry," because industry-wide rules force them to

bear the full weight of paperwork requirements or other mandated procedures designed to catch the irresponsible firms causing much of the problem. Case-by-case enforcement is different. It focuses on the malefactors in an industry. . . . It is much harder for a malefactor to convince a congressional committee that the FTC action is unjust when the facts reveal a clear abuse; by contrast, in a rulemaking, the industry has available a range of respectable and genuinely responsible members who can come forth to tell how they are aggrieved by the burdens of a proposed FTC rule.[105]

The FTC's turn toward case-by-case adjudication, combined with its adoption of high standards for justifying its rulemaking activities, led it to terminate many of the rules that were under consideration in the early 1980s.[106]

Even in its resurgence as an activist agency in the late 1980s, the FTC demonstrated that it had learned its political lessons well. When President Bush appointed Janet Steiger to chair the FTC in 1989, Washington antitrust lawyers and policy watchers announced that "the old FTC lion is starting to rouse again—and roar."[107] They noted that Steiger's tough speeches on consumer protection issues "augur coming changes in the deregulatory dogma propounded by the Reagan Administration."[108] Indeed, the "surge in antitrust and consumer-protection enforcement actions under Chairwoman Janet Steiger" has sent a clear "message to business that the no-go stance of the past decade is over."[109] Yet, Steiger's activism has consisted solely of increasing the FTC's law-enforcement functions. With neither the political will nor the legal authority to return to the "go-go activism of the late 1970s," the resurgent FTC has found little use for its Magnuson-Moss rulemaking powers.

Empirical analysis of the workings of the FTC legislative veto shows that the Reagan administration's crusade against FTC activism does not fully explain why the mechanism was irrelevant to policy outcomes. It shows that the mechanism was politically significant only as a symbol of congressional oversight. It also shows that the mechanism lost this symbolic power as the FTC learned to avoid exercising its delegated powers in as freewheeling a manner as it did in the mid-1970s. The actual restraints imposed by Congress on the agency's rulemaking powers consisted of extensive public participation requirements and an extremely wide scope of review of agency rules granted to the courts. Together, by drawing into the political process widespread objections to the FTC's freewheeling exercise of its regulatory powers, these mechanisms forced the agency to adopt legal restrictions on its rulemaking authorities and to turn away from rulemaking activities to case-by-case adjudications.

CONCLUSION

Had members been successful in passing a generic legislative veto bill rather than simply enacting a veto provision into the FTC Act, then the veto mechanism might not have been doomed to irrelevance. Though the FTC's retreat from ill-conceived regulatory policies undermined the legislative veto's symbolic power by the early 1980s, other agencies were undoubtedly exercising their powers in ways that could certainly have rekindled members' desire to flaunt legislative veto authority. Without a generic veto, however, members could only threaten to exercise the legislative veto over offending regulations that were being proposed pursuant to statutes with veto provisions already enacted into them.[110] Supporters of the generic bill thus cautioned that "if we don't adopt a generic legislative veto bill that would bring some uniformity and predictability to this whole process, these [provisions] will simply continue to proliferate piecemeal in all manner of forms," thereby rendering the veto mechanism, through "confusion" and "chaos," difficult to use.[111]

But Congress never enacted a generic legislative veto bill. Committee chairs, as well as members of the House Rules Committee, quietly objected to the mechanism because it threatened to empower backbenchers intent on thwarting the will of congressional leaders.[112] In addition, both President Carter and President Reagan promised to veto any generic legislative veto bill that would allow members to bypass the constitutional requirement of presentment to the president. Nonetheless, both generic veto bills that came to a vote in Congress received broad support.[113] So while it is unlikely that further attempts at passing such a bill would have been successful, it would have continued to remain a possibility if the Supreme Court in *Chadha* had not declared the legislative veto unequivocally unconstitutional. *Chadha* was perhaps most significant, therefore, in eliminating the possibility that Congress would ever grant itself a generic legislative veto.

The Supreme Court's enforcement of separation of powers procedures was of little consequence in the case of the FTC veto because the FTC's exercise of its delegated powers was not affected by the presence of legislative veto authority. This exercise, instead, evolved in response to vociferous criticisms by members and their constituents, demands imposed by judicial review, and changes in administration policy. Thus, the irrelevance of the FTC veto provides a detailed example of how American political institutions are capable of reversing unsuccessful administrative policies.

The principles underlying this capacity for institutional evolution are articulated in the *Federalist Papers,* in Publius's discussion of the interdependence between representation and effective governance embodied in the separation of powers system. He expects that American government, which is "wholly popular," will tend to reverse ineffective uses of its administrative powers because the people's "confidence in and obedience to a government will commonly be proportioned to the goodness or badness of its administration."[114] This obviously does not guarantee that such reversals will occur quickly enough or often enough to ensure that the government will retain the confidence of the people. What it does suggest, and what the irrelevance of the FTC veto provides evidence to support, is that the American political system clearly is not dependent on shortcuts through constitutional procedure to restrain a politically inastute agency from exercising its powers unwisely.

Chapter Five

LEGISLATIVE VETOES IN EDUCATION STATUTES

The legislative vetoes in education statutes are among the most important and most powerful of the veto provisions ever enacted over executive branch regulatory authorities. "To the Office of Education (OE) goes the dubious distinction," in fact, "of being the first federal agency to have its rulemaking authority subject to the legislative veto."[1] In addition, the legislative vetoes governing education regulations, in contrast to other areas, were comprehensive and generic, in that they were applicable to almost all of the programs administered by OE (which was renamed the Department of Education in 1980).[2] To those scholars who believed that the invention of the legislative veto had significantly altered interbranch relations, the effect of *Chadha* on the unusually large scope of the education statute veto provisions promised to weaken congressional control over policymaking at the Department of Education (ED).

THE CONVENTIONAL WISDOM

Scholars and commentators have had good reason to expect the loss of the legislative veto to alter outcomes in education policymaking. Members on the education committees themselves expressed concern about having lost an important control mechanism. In addition, legislative histories of the education statutes containing veto provisions—the Education Amendments of 1972 governing the new financial aid program for higher education (Pell Grants), and the General Education Provisions Act (GEPA) of 1974 governing the other regulatory activities of OE—show that members enacted these provisions because they mistrusted the administration's education policies. Furthermore, existing studies of the workings of these statutes claim that the veto provisions played an essential role in protecting congressional policy prerogatives.

Members' indignation at the Supreme Court's invalidation of the veto mechanism led them to rescind the authority of the secretary of education to promulgate the needs analysis formulas, referred to as "family contribution schedules," for the Pell Grant program. The loss of the veto provision attached to the Pell Grant program, members argued, would "greatly constrain the ability of the Congress to ensure that the administration of student aid programs conforms to the legislative intent in their enactment."[3] To avoid this dangerous situation, explained the committee report attached to the law in which the secretary's authority was rescinded, Congress would henceforth provide for family contribution schedules in statute.[4]

Members expressed similar concerns about the loss of the legislative veto in GEPA. This is evident from the recent proliferation in education statutes of mandatory "negotiated rulemaking" provisions. These regulatory negotiations, or "reg negs," "bring together representatives of the agency and the various interest groups to negotiate the text of a proposed rule" before that rule is published in the *Federal Register*.[5] In so doing, reg negs make the affected communities of state and local education officials, and of parents and teachers, better able to participate in the regulatory process. Members have demanded that ED exhibit greater responsiveness to these communities because of "the absence of a previous congressional authority known as a legislative veto over final regulations."[6]

Members enacted the innovative veto mechanism into both the Pell Grant and GEPA statutes in the early 1970s because they were concerned about protecting congressional policymaking prerogatives. In developing the Pell Grant program, members agreed with the Nixon administration that federal funds for students pursuing higher education should be distributed according to a "standardized determination." No such standardization was yet in place, however, because existing campus-based financial aid programs distributed funds according to criteria developed by various private associations.[7] Committed to endowing OE with the authorities necessary to set up a new student financial aid program, members delegated to the agency the responsibility for producing a standardized annual needs analysis schedule.

But interbranch acrimony between the Democrats on the education committees and the Republicans in the White House made members reluctant to lodge such a powerful public policy instrument in the executive branch.[8] Changing the needs analysis formulas defining the standardized determination would naturally "alter the number and type of students eligible for grants, the maximum award and the purchasing power of Pell Grants relative to college costs."[9] To show that they intended to prevent the administration from using the needs analysis schedules as a policy instrument, members enacted a legislative veto into the Pell Grant statute. The provision authorized either chamber, through a majority resolution, to disapprove the needs analysis schedules proposed by OE.[10]

The legislative veto in GEPA also represented a safeguard of congressional policy views. The administration helped foment mistrust in Congress in the early 1970s by attempting to use its budgetary authority to undermine the policies enacted in the 1972 Education Act. Its student aid package in the budget submitted immediately following passage of the 1972 legislation ran directly counter to congressional intentions. Though the legislation explicitly required that the existing campus-based financial aid programs be continued at specified minimum levels, the administration's budget called for phasing out the old programs to help finance the new Pell Grant program.[11] In response, the appropriations committees completely rearranged the administration's budget to fit with original congressional intent—they granted the Pell Grant program such a small appropriation, in fact, that the education committees had to pass a separate resolution restricting eligibility for the program's first year.

Members' mistrust of the administration's education policy was also fueled by OE's diversion of appropriated funds to programs not directly authorized by Congress. The most outspoken critic of this practice, Senator Alan Cranston (D-CA), complained that "without benefit of legislation, the Commissioner has begun siphoning off Upward Bound funds for the Right to Read program. The Right to Read program has admirable goals with which I agree; however, it ought to be funded separately under specific legislation and not by funds appropriated for other purposes."[12]

To examine and focus attention on the administration's violation of congressional policy prerogatives, the House Committee on Education and Labor held hearings in 1973. The testimony in these hearings confirmed and extended interbranch hostility. To Secretary Frank Carlucci's statement that "I accept with good grace your criticism . . . ," for example, Rep. William Ford (D-MI) shot back, "I don't want you to accept with good grace. I think the Office of Education is at the lowest level since I have been in Congress."[13]

Sensitive to the extremely hostile character of these hearings, Rep. John Brademas (D-IN) explained that

> I have been very rough on you today, but I don't have the kind of trouble with my Republican colleagues on the Committee that I have with you in the executive branch. . . . If you detect a big chip on our shoulder, it is because, in my judgment, the mentality that led to Watergate, the mentality of which Mr. Dean has been testifying, "the do it yourself lawyers, you do anything you want to do," runs throughout the Department of HEW. . . . We are not being partisan. . . . This administration . . . has to learn that we in Congress are a coequal branch of the U.S. Government and that we got elected too.[14]

Carlucci concluded that "as I reflect on this hearing . . . I think there are differences of views that have emerged. There are perhaps differences in interpretation, understandable differences. But, quite frankly, words like 'fraudulent, deceptive, integrity, Watergate, felony,' those are very strong words."[15] Brademas assured him that "they were meant to be."[16]

THE EDUCATION VETOES IN CONTEXT

Enacted in the midst of intense interbranch hostility, the veto provisions in education statutes were prime examples of members' intent to increase their oversight of policy implementation. When these provisions are examined within the larger context of executive-legislative relations generally, however, with attention to the variety of sources of congressional oversight authority, it becomes clear that the legislative veto was inconsequential to Congress's impressive power to control the administration of education policy.

Sources of Congressional Oversight Power

Statutory reporting requirements have long proven to be an essential source of congressional oversight power in education policymaking. As the size and number of federal education programs began to explode in the late 1960s and early 1970s, Congress became increasingly dissatisfied with OE's unpredictable exercise of its regulatory powers. Unlike most regulatory agencies, OE was not subject to the requirements of the Administrative Procedure Act (APA) to engage the public in the development of rules.[17] The APA exempts federal grant distribution activities from the notice-and-comment rulemaking procedures meant to ensure public participation.[18] But OE caused widespread congressional frustration when it began to implement the massive program, initiated by the Elementary and Secondary Education Act of 1965, of grants-in-aid to state and local educational institutions.[19] Free from the constraints of the APA, OE began administering these aid programs "under unpublished rules or without any rules at all."[20]

Congressional dissatisfaction grew with the growing number of affected groups that had to contend with sporadic publication of regulations. These groups did not even have easy access to those regulations that OE did publish. When they were published, they "appeared in the form of guidelines, handbooks and even internal memoranda; they were not published in the *Federal Register*."[21] In response to complaints from their constituents, members began to subject OE's activities to strict scrutiny. In addition to confirming existing suspicions of "serious irregularities" in the manner in which OE distributed grants, congressional scrutiny found that OE had an "abysmal records system." Thus, not only was it difficult for affected groups to understand the criteria by which OE intended to award grants, but it was "almost impossible" for them to "obtain accurate information—or even sketchy information, for that matter—on such questions as what projects are currently being funded, what projects have recently been completed, what contractors or grantees hold which contracts or grants."[22]

Legislative vetoes were only one piece of a whole set of statutory responses to OE's ad hoc use of its powers. The more important pieces were two provisions enacted in 1970 specifically intended to fulfill members' demands for increased access to OE's regulatory decision-making. Of these two provisions, one OE official explained, the one that most vitally affected the life of the agency was the Pucinski amendment, which required that OE publish any "rules, regulations, . . . or requirements of general applicability prescribed . . . for the administration of any applicable program" in the *Federal Register,* and that no such rules or regulations take effect until thirty days after publication.[23] By mandating that OE publish all proposed regulatory activities before putting them into effect, the Pucinski amendment forced OE to subject its proposed activities to the opinions of members of Congress and all interested members of the public.[24]

The other statutory requirement enacted in 1970, the Green amendment, was explicitly directed at overseeing OE's statutory interpretation. It required that all "'rules, regulations, guidelines or other published interpretations or orders' issued by [OE] . . . must contain immediately following each substantive provision . . . [citations to the] legal authority upon which the provision is based."[25]

Forced to comply with comprehensive reporting requirements, OE quickly ceased operating like a loose cannon. The agency chose to begin abiding by APA public comment procedures for all of its regulatory activities soon after the enactment of the Pucinski and Green amendments.[26] Members were wary, however, of trusting that the agency under the Nixon administration would voluntarily stick to APA rulemaking procedures, so they imposed extensive legal constraints on OE. They converted the 30-day hold on regulations enacted in 1970 into a directive that OE utilize the APA notice-and-comment procedures.[27] In addition, the 1974 amendments to GEPA subjected OE rules to a unique 45-day waiting period, imposed a 240-day time limit on OE's rulemaking process, and required that OE notify Congress of the timetable by which it intended to complete the rulemaking process for all proposed regulations.[28]

The deeply felt ambivalence in American political culture toward entrusting the federal government with policymaking power over education issues helped ensure that these statutory reporting requirements would force the administration to pay close attention to congressional opinions.[29] Since education has always been jealously guarded by local communities as an issue rightfully theirs to control, members have explicitly protected the policymaking power of local communities in every major law authorizing the government to engage in education activities.[30] They have also made sure that OE, and later ED, have had little discretion to develop programs not authorized by legislation.[31] By making federal education officials highly dependent on Congress for approval of even the smallest policy experiments or innovations, the deep-seated mistrust of federal education activities strengthened the policymaking power of statutory reporting requirements. Once members had the opportunity to express their opinions on proposed education regulations, administrators were unlikely to ignore them.

Together with statutory reporting requirements, Congress's lawmaking power has served as a key source of members' control of ED's implementation of education statutes. When, for example, the Nixon administration attempted to zero out the campus-based financial aid programs because it wanted to focus federal funds on the Pell Grant program, Congress simply responded by requiring, in statute, that the Pell Grant program be inaugurated only after the campus-based programs had been funded. In addition, Congress appropriated less money for the Pell Grant program than the administration expected. By making good use of their lawmaking power, members have ensured that their substantive policy differences with the administration have consistently resulted in "congressional dominance and executive branch irrelevance."[32]

Though it is rather self-evident that Congress's lawmaking authority is an important source of congressional oversight power, it is nonetheless necessary to demonstrate the practical significance of this power. The legislative veto mechanism acquired a reputation as an important policymaking tool precisely because it authorized members to shortcut the supposedly unwieldy lawmaking process. As the case of the Pell Grant program shows, however, members often chose to use the full legislative process to overturn proposed policy even though they had the option of using legislative vetoes.

When the Reagan administration first took office, it proposed a 30 percent cut in the Pell Grant program.[33] Instead of using the Consumer Price Index to calculate annual updates for grant programs, recalled one staff member at ED responsible for postsecondary programs, Office of Management and Budget (OMB) Director David Stockman decided to use a more conservative inflator. This naturally resulted in smaller grant sizes. But it was never implemented because "Congress said 'no way.' They just passed a law that voided our use of the OMB inflator."[34]

The Pell Grant program had evolved into a program with strong congressional support during the 1970s. By 1981 the Pell Grants had become, along with the even larger Guaranteed Student Loans (GSL) for middle-income students, one of "the fastest-growing programs in the federal budget."[35] A key change in 1978, Congress's enactment of the Middle Income Student Assistance Act (MISAA), made the Pell Grant program one of the most popular and widely supported programs in Congress. The MISAA grew out of pressure that had begun to mount in the mid-1970s to broaden the base of eligibility for student aid, "for some kind of response to the 'middle-income squeeze' in financing college costs."[36] The MISAA liberalized eligibility for Pell Grants and opened GSL loans to any student regardless of income or need. It increased student aid for higher education by almost 40 percent in one year, and increased the number of students receiving aid from three million to five million. The MISAA, Rep. Ford exclaimed happily, was "the single biggest infusion of funding for middle income students since the adoption of the GI Bill at the end of World War II."[37]

The expanded Pell Grant program acquired bipartisan support so quickly that Reagan administration officials themselves admitted, in 1981, that their proposed cuts were somewhat radical. "The administration witness at the subcommittee hearing characterized its own schedule as 'relatively harsh,'" Senator Robert Stafford (R-VT) noted, in calling for a reversal of the president's proposed cuts. "I would characterize it as 'regressive,' as it imposes, at a minimum, a 40 percent assessment, or tax rate, on family discretionary income, virtually four times that imposed in the last schedule submitted. This assessment is so high as to eliminate students with adjusted gross family incomes above $15,000 from the program—effectively repealing the Middle Income Student Assistance Act of 1978."[38]

Reagan's attempt to slash the Pell Grant program was dashed when Congress, through the appropriations process, enacted a family contribution schedule that preserved the eligibility requirements of the previous year. Senator Stafford's amendment, which "put in place the same schedule as last year, adjusted for inflation and other updated changes," had the effect of "precluding . . . the implementation of the admittedly unreasonable family contribution schedule sent to Congress by the administration on October 13, after a delay of more than 6 weeks."[39] Stafford's amendment did not make for a particularly elegant appropriations bill, for, as his critics noted, it was "clearly legislation and really should not be offered as part of an appropriations bill."[40] Even those who objected on these procedural grounds, however, accepted Stafford's amendment "because of the urgent need for this."[41] "By delaying," explained Rep. Paul Simon (D-IL), "the administration figures [it] will discourage some kids from going to college and would save some money."[42]

Reagan subsequently vetoed the omnibus appropriations bill containing Stafford's amendment, claiming that it was "a budget-busting appropriations bill that would finance the entire Government at levels well above my recommendations, and thus set back our efforts to halt the excessive Government spending that has fueled inflation. . . . I asked for a reduction of 12% in the appropriations for nearly all non-defense discretionary programs. . . . The 12% cut would have saved $8.5 billion."[43] The reworked bill that finally passed, however, left the Stafford amendment untouched. Reagan continued to propose cuts in the Pell Grant program, but Congress continued to enact the family contribution schedules into law. Reagan never singled out these Pell Grant schedules as a reason to veto any bills, however, because he "read the tea leaves in the House and Senate," Rep. Simon explained, and realized that "his veto would have been overwhelmingly overridden."[44] Thus, "reports of the death of student aid were greatly exaggerated in 1981–82; public and congressional reaction quelled any notion that federal commitments in this area would be deserted."[45]

If the Pell Grant schedules were subject to a one-house veto, and there was deep sentiment within Congress that the administration's proposed schedules were unacceptable, why did members not exercise their legislative veto authority? In fact, on one occasion, they did. Observing the context in which this occurred shows why the veto mechanism was of little use to the committees in terms of policy control. When ED proposed its first family contribution schedule under the Reagan administration, the Senate passed a one-house veto disapproving the schedule.[46] Practically speaking, however, this resolution was unnecessary because Congress enacted its own version of a family contribution schedule into law. The legislative veto resolution did little more than "complement" Congress's incorporation of the Stafford amendment into law.[47]

If members had wanted to rely solely on the legislative veto to reach their preferred policy outcome, they would have had to continue vetoing the administration's schedules until it produced one they deemed acceptable. In this way, members would have been much less certain to achieve their objective than if they enacted their desired schedules into law. Nothing would have pleased the Reagan administration more than to have members continually veto proposed schedules, because without approved schedules, no funds could have been distributed. Members naturally decided not to rely on the veto mechanism. Instead, they fixed "the terms and conditions of the Family Contribution Schedule for Pell Grants and the Guaranteed Student Loan program for the 1983–84 academic year, in order to mitigate the current disruption in planning and to prevent additional problems for students and their families."[48] Throughout the 1980s, in fact, Congress protected its Pell Grant policy objectives through its lawmaking authority—by annually enacting the family contribution schedules into law.

The Scope of the Legislative Veto

Studies that represent the education vetoes as an important source of congressional oversight power overlook the significance of statutory reporting requirements and of Congress's lawmaking power.[49] This mistake rests in defining "legislative veto" too broadly. The "legislative veto" examined by existing studies includes functions that go beyond the veto's actual shortcut of constitutional procedure. But there is good reason why many scholars have exaggerated the scope of the mechanism.

When first enacted into education statutes in the early 1970s, the "legislative veto" was generally understood to include the reporting and waiting requirements attached to it. The 45-day waiting period associated with the legislative veto in GEPA, for example, was originally understood to be as much a part of the veto mechanism as the constitutional innovation that specifically endowed Congress with the power to disapprove regulations by concurrent resolution. Describing the GEPA legislative veto soon after it was created, one legal scholar explained that "affected rules were to be transmitted to Congress and were to take effect forty-five days later unless disapproved in the meantime by concurrent resolution of both Houses. . . . The Department has complied with this requirement despite doubts about its constitutionality."[50] The department's compliance with the statutory reporting requirement and 45-day waiting period served as evidence, in this scholar's mind, that members were exercising their legislative veto authority.

By failing to articulate carefully the specific technical characteristics of the legislative veto struck down by the Supreme Court, scholars and commentators expected the invalidation of the mechanism to undo ED's regular reporting to Congress.[51] Had the court's decision invalidated statutory reporting requirements, it would have most certainly driven a knife into the heart of congressional oversight power. Yet the court only invalidated those parts of the "legislative veto" that violated the bicameralism and presentment clauses. Only those provisions that allowed one or both houses to veto a proposed regulation without the president's signature were objectionable in the court's opinion. Statutory reporting requirements remained untouched in the court's demolition of the veto mechanism. An attorney in the ED general counsel's office explained that *Chadha* provided no freedom from congressional oversight because in response to the court's action "we just continued business as usual. Business *would* have really changed if *Chadha* had said that Congress can no longer require us to report everything. But—unfortunately for us—it didn't."[52]

Congressional Oversight at Work

Since the legislative veto never served as a significant oversight tool, its invalidation did not weaken congressional power to exercise control over policy outcomes. In the case of the Pell Grant needs analysis schedules, for example, members continued to express their disagreements with ED policies in the same manner as when legislative veto authority had been available to them. In the first student aid bill passed after the veto's invalidation, Congress simply followed its own precedent of enacting family contribution schedules into law, and enacted new schedules for the 1984–85 and 1985–86 academic years.[53] In its first opportunity to reauthorize the Pell Grant program, furthermore, Congress codified its practice of enacting needs analysis schedules into law by formally rescinding the secretary's authority to even attempt to promulgate schedules.[54]

The workings of the GEPA reporting requirements also demonstrate that the legislative veto's invalidation did not weaken congressional oversight power. One of the most acrimonious of interbranch policy disagreements under GEPA involved regulations intended to tighten student loan rules.[55] As soon as he took office as the new secretary of education, William Bennett chose to make these rules a priority of his regulatory policy. Any issue so chosen by Bennett was sure to involve him in a highly visible and controversial policy struggle with the incumbent Democrats on the education committees, because Bennett was one of the most vocal and articulate of the ideological "movement conservatives" of the Reagan administration.[56] Bennett's confirmation hearings had barely ended, in fact, before he became the target of great hostility within Congress.[57] He explicitly defended the administration's intent to "'cut to the bone' and eventually eliminate all federal financial assistance to education."[58]

Bennett intended to penalize schools with high student loan default rates because "defaults in the GSL program cost taxpayers $1.3 billion in fiscal 1987 and an estimated $1.6 billion in fiscal 1988."[59] But any attempt to prevent such schools from receiving additional federal funds was bound to elicit virulent objections because most of the problematic institutions were either historically black colleges or proprietary schools.[60] Benjamin Payton, president of the historically black Tuskegee University, branded Bennett's policy as threatening to unjustly penalize institutions for something over which they had no control.[61] Noting that proprietary schools (for-profit trade schools) serve students from the lowest socioeconomic background, a student aid consultant predicted that such schools would be highly unlikely to meet any of Bennett's requirements.[62] As a result, Bennett would find himself "in for a big fight" if he attempted to make good on his threats.

Notwithstanding the concerns of the education community, Bennett put strong teeth in his threat to clamp down on schools with high default rates. In 1988, ED formally proposed a set of rules that would make institutions with student default rates of more than 20 percent ineligible for federal student loan programs.[63] In proposing these regulations, ED declared that it intended to turn a deaf ear to institutions that stood most to lose by these regulations. It announced that "the Department does not consider the composition of the student body admitted by an institution to be an acceptable explanation for a high default rate."[64]

As soon as the proposed regulations were published, the OMB official responsible for overseeing them recalled that "a flurry of bills was proposed to legislate over the regs, and ED got close to 3000 comments!"[65] The legislation drafted by members in response to the uproar caused by Bennett's regulations "put less of a burden on the schools to assure loan repayment."[66] It was never enacted because there was no consensus, either in the education community or among members, about how stringent the rules governing loan defaults should be.[67] Members were certain, however, that Bennett's proposed regulations were too stringent. Consequently, they demanded that ED extend the comment period on the regulations in order to give the higher education community time to work out a viable solution.[68] Members' demonstrated willingness to legislate over ED's regulatory authority convinced the department to back away from its policy on loan defaults.

In extending the comment period on the student loan default rules, ED made the substance of its policy open to negotiation with members and interested groups. Members began to "float . . . some less stringent proposals" to ED, such as requiring trade schools with high default rates to come up with special corrective measures without necessarily barring them from participating in federal student assistance programs.[69] Many of those who had been most opposed to Bennett's stringent regulations began to acknowledge, once brought into the policymaking process, that "clearly there's a problem with student loan defaults that can't be allowed to continue," and "something has to be done."[70] These interest groups believed the extended comment period to have made it possible to "work with [ED] to develop good regulations on the default situation."[71]

Once Bennett agreed to extend the comment period on proposed student loan default regulations, he essentially conceded defeat of one of his priority policy objectives. The extension gave members and constituent groups the opportunity to work with ED officials to alter the substance of Bennett's proposed regulations. Bennett had earlier ignored their attempts to make his highly controversial regulations more palatable because he was intent on imposing stringent penalties. In his attempt to develop regulations without any input from groups that stood to be affected by them, however, he provoked an outcry that immediately led members to force open the rulemaking process.

Controversies over the validation of data for student loan applications represent a possible counterexample to the picture drawn here of congressional oversight at work. In contrast to the case of the loan default regulations, ED succeeded in issuing final regulations governing data validation even though these violated the policy preferences of influential members and powerful interest groups. ED had traditionally gathered the information necessary for calculating a student's need and expected family contribution by having students fill out forms. In response to several studies showing that this information was sometimes inaccurate, the department in 1978–79 initiated a "validation" method for checking student data.[72] In 1981, a report on that year's Pell Grant program showed that information errors resulted in an estimated $563 million worth of overawards or underawards.[73] To minimize these errors, ED proposed a large increase in the number of validations it would require on-campus financial aid offices to conduct for 1982–83.[74]

Members disapproved of this increase because their constituents felt that "such drastic measures are uncalled for at this time. Our fear is these procedures will create unnecessary hardships on the very students and programs they are primarily designed to serve."[75] As a member of the House Education and Labor Committee, Rep. Simon was especially vocal in opposing ED's proposed validation increase, claiming that its methods "imposed costs on schools but did not necessarily reduce award errors."[76]

Secretary Bennett was nonetheless "committed to tightening up the verification of data on student loan applications," one OMB official recalled.[77] Bennett proposed regulations that required institutions to verify 100 percent of the student loan applications that were in some way error-prone. In response, many financial aid administrators complained that they were already overburdened with paperwork, and warned that further requirements to verify loan applications "would slow the process even more but would not produce significant savings for the government."[78] In spite of these comments, ED implemented final regulations that retained the 100 percent verification requirement. ED explained its decision by stating, simply, that "no change has been made. An application that . . . may contain error . . . must be verified."[79]

The case of the data verification regulations is clearly one where Bennett flew directly in the face of strong public and congressional opposition, turning his unpopular proposed regulations into final regulations rather than agreeing to negotiation and compromise. But his success at disregarding the opinions elicited during reporting periods proved to be his undoing. Precisely because he was able to implement his controversial regulations without paying much attention to the views of affected groups, Bennett outraged members who represented these groups. Indignant at having been cut out of the regulatory process, these members were easily able to obtain the necessary support of their colleagues to legislate over such regulations.

"Bennett got people angry," explained an OMB official, "because he was determined to implement these regs irrespective of the experiences of people in the field. So Congress just responded by capping in legislation the verification percentage at 30."[80] Congress formally overturned ED's regulations in the 1986 Higher Education Act Reauthorization with a provision expressly prohibiting institutions from verifying the data of more than 30 percent of the applicants in any award year.[81] Bennett's unusual decision to implement final regulations without consulting members or affected groups on the substance of those regulations proved to be a pyrrhic victory.

Observing ED's attempts to bypass reporting requirements altogether provides further evidence of the policymaking power that resides in these requirements. In a controversy over race-based scholarships during the Bush administration, ED's top civil rights official, Michael Williams, declared race-specific scholarships unconstitutional. Since he did not initiate "formal regulatory procedures," which would have required him to publish his policy statement as an Advanced Notice of Proposed Rulemaking in the *Federal Register*, critics stated that Williams's statement "should be viewed as no more than his own personal opinion."[82]

In hastily called congressional hearings on the matter, Rep. Ted Weiss (D-NY) angrily took Williams to task for bypassing reporting requirements, exclaiming that "in this mad rush to ban minority scholarships, you violated the Administrative Procedure Act . . . an Act [meant] to avoid just such a situation, where laws are changed in secret, without public notice."[83] ED officials attempted to justify Williams's avoidance of notice-and-comment procedures by arguing that the Office of Civil Rights (OCR) was not subject to APA requirements:

> Policy decisions by the Secretary of HEW, to publish HEW policy in the *Federal Register* are not, in my view, binding on the Secretary of Education. After the Department of Education was formed in 1980, to the best of my knowledge, no Secretary of Education has published such a notice saying that the Office for Civil Rights would only issue policy through publication in the *Federal Register*.[84]

This fact garnered little attention on Capitol Hill. Irrespective of whether members had expected OCR to comply with APA notice-and-comment procedures in the past, the debate on race-based scholarships turned to whether Williams's pronouncement represented a change in policy. If it did represent a change, then members would demand that it be subjected to the public comment procedures required by the APA. Thus, ED tried to justify its evasion of public consultation by claiming that "we have not proposed any change to our existing regulations, nor do we consider anything that Mr. Williams said . . . as being inconsistent with the existing regulations."[85] But this argument also failed to carry much weight on the Hill, so ED ultimately deferred to congressional demands that it subject its controversial policy proposal to notice-and-comment procedures.[86]

Several months later, after having been subjected to public comment procedures, ED's proposed regulations on race-based scholarships were a much watered-down version of Williams's original statement. Williams had announced that no federal funds could be used for such scholarships. Though the revised regulations did not allow schools to create separate "race-based" categories for awards, it explicitly allowed them to "come up with more complex criteria for scholarships. . . . Rather than tailoring scholarships to blacks, schools could award them on, say, a flexible point system—making 'need' 1 point, 'academics' 1 point, and 'race' 2 points."[87] Since schools could continue to use race as a valid category, therefore, the proposed policy change did not amount to much of a change.[88] ED's various attempts to avoid reporting requirements for Williams's policy statement were grounded in a solid understanding of the power of such requirements to affect policy outcomes.[89] Once forced to comply with them, ED knew full well that it would have to give up all hope of implementing Williams's original policy statement.

Knowing also that the legislative veto's invalidation left statutory reporting requirements in place, and was irrelevant to Congress's constitutional authority to pass, and threaten to pass, laws, ED officials, unlike political scientists, did not expect it to alter the balance of policymaking power between the branches.

THE LEGISLATIVE VETO'S IMPACT ON THE POLICYMAKING PROCESS

Existing studies wrongly assume that legislative veto authority to shortcut the constitutionally mandated procedures for legislative action increased congressional control over policy outcomes. Consequently, they fail to explore the possibility that the mechanism affected the legislative process in ways other than by shifting the balance of policymaking power between the branches. Exploring this other possibility shows that ridding education statutes of the legislative veto shortcut made it easier for members to fulfill their representative functions.

Pell Grant Statute

Congress's retraction of the secretary's authority to promulgate needs analysis schedules—a direct response to the Supreme Court's invalidation of the legislative veto—had no effect on policy outcomes. This retraction simply codified what had already been, for several years, Congress's routine practice of enacting needs analysis schedules into law. Nonetheless, the formal elimination of this authority left a significant mark on the Pell Grant program because the success of the program is so dependent on stability. "Any formula-driven grant program," explained one lobbyist from the American Council of Education, "has got to have some sort of stability. It would be ridiculous if a whole bunch of students would all of a sudden be eligible for grant money one year and then ineligible the next."[90] If the government decides that smaller, or larger, or differently characterized populations should be eligible for particular grant monies, she continued,

> the changes in the formulas that are used to distribute these monies should be discussed and considered in the open: with direct attention to the policy reasons for and against the proposed changes. But for the federal government to make such changes by playing around with the formulas here and there, year after year, is unfair. The government can't be so whimsical to parents, to students, to financial aid administrators, to taxpayers.[91]

Stability and predictability in the needs analysis formulas, in other words, are of central importance to the operation of the Pell Grant program. "Pell is not a total entitlement program since it requires Congress to set appropriations levels every year," she explained, "but it's pretty close. It's a semi-entitlement program. It's formula-driven so the institutions out there expect to be able to predict how much money their students will receive," she concluded, re-emphasizing that "it doesn't make sense for the government to have private internal debates about what the formulas are going to be every year."[92]

By endowing the administration with the authority to promulgate needs analysis schedules, the Pell Grant statute left open the possibility that eligibility criteria for the program might change from one year to the next without public deliberation. This possibility became especially problematic when the arrival of the Reagan administration brought a concerted effort to exclude middle- and lower middle-class students from the program. But members jealously guarded the stability of the Pell Grant program because they did not want large numbers of constituents to suddenly become ineligible for participation.

Describing the deep commitment within Congress to the program, one higher education lobbyist noted that "Republicans were just as vehemently opposed to letting the administration play around with delays and formula changes as the Democrats on the Hill."[93] So they overturned the administration's attempts to alter the size of the program by enacting, easily and immediately, their own schedules into statute.

By rescinding the secretary's authority, Congress guaranteed that Pell Grant program policy would no longer change without the large-scale, visible deliberations characteristic of the legislative reauthorization process. Since "the administration no longer futzes around year after year with the schedules,"[94] the higher education lobbyist continued to explain, financial aid officers and high-school guidance counselors are much better able to advise students "in a timely and informed manner . . . about the availability of federal student aid."[95] Congress's rescinding of the secretary's authority has also made the Pell Grant program less costly. One of the staff members of the House Education Committee explained that

> financial aid administrators have started to use big computer programs to systematize their implementation of Pell. And they can get hooked up to the legislation, so once they set up the computer program, all they have to do is get the annual updates in the data, like the inflation multiplier and the maximum Pell Grant award, and then they're all set. Imagine if they had to factor in the possibility that the secretary might alter the needs analysis formulas from one year to the next. Then they'd have to throw out the whole program and spend thousands of dollars to set up a new one.[96]

The legislative veto in the Pell Grant statute never played a significant role in affecting policy outcomes, but its invalidation helped goad members into rescinding the secretary's authority to propose needs analysis schedules. In so doing, the invalidation of the legislative veto minimized the costs associated with annual policy wars between the elected branches. The absence of legislative veto authority was of direct consequence to the policymaking process, therefore, because it forced members to take full statutory responsibility for their unflinching support of the Pell Grant program.

GEPA

The response of members to the loss of the legislative veto in GEPA provides further evidence that absence of legislative veto authority carried noteworthy consequences for the policymaking process. Since the education committees first mandated that ED engage in a reg neg to develop regulations for the 1988 amendments to the Elementary and Secondary Education Act, members have anointed the procedure as the substitute for the invalidated legislative veto.[97]

Both mechanisms became popular because members wanted to force ED to make its regulatory process more open to the public. When they enacted the legislative veto into GEPA in 1974, OE had just begun to abide by the public comment procedures of the APA after years of unpredictable and somewhat secretive rulemaking. Though ED has since continued to abide by these APA requirements, the Reagan administration's hostility to the education community led interested groups to demand greater access to all stages of ED's regulatory process. This demand, combined with the Supreme Court's invalidation of the legislative veto, made members eager to find a new procedural mechanism they could insert in statutes to signal their responsiveness. Reg negs proved the perfect solution because those in the education community who had participated in reg-neg procedures advocated them enthusiastically.[98]

Much like the legislative vetoes they replaced, the new reg-neg procedures in education statutes have been insignificant to Congress's control of policy outcomes. Thus, for example, the 1988 reg neg had "no impact on the proposed regulations. . . . The process did not ensure a consensus on the major issues, its prime objective, and [it] resulted in few consensus agreements."[99] One of the debates it helped resolve, recalled one of the OMB participants in the process, was "whether a particular regulation should use the verb 'convene' instead of 'meet.'"[100] The major policy controversies were resolved through standard mechanisms and procedures. "Because the negotiators were unable to reach consensus on so many issues related to these services," explained the *Federal Register* notice following the Vocational Education Act reg neg, "the Secretary particularly invites further comments on these provisions."[101]

Despite their lack of policy consequence, reg negs have remained extremely popular among members. To critics of the procedure, this popularity reflects the congressional naïveté about the regulatory process. One ED official who worked closely with the participants in all of the department's reg negs could "not understand why the Hill wants to keep requiring us to do these reg negs. Maybe you do reach a consensus on some issues. But even if you do, no one is required to live by it. Neither the department nor the interest groups themselves are bound by anything that goes on in those negotiations."[102] An OMB official who was similarly perplexed attributed the popularity of reg negs to members' mistaken assumption that the procedure restricts ED's regulatory authorities. "I think reg negs are popular," he explained, "because Congress forgets that the department is a negotiator in the process too. They forget that the department has the authority to say 'no, we don't agree with this' even if all the other negotiators around the table reach consensus on something."[103]

Finding it implausible that members could be unaware of executive branch powers, one ED official gave a different explanation for the popularity of reg negs. He spoke, instead, of the "PR," or public relations value of the procedure:

> Our reg negs are not really negotiated rulemakings because in the end, we can do whatever we want. We're not legally bound and everyone knows that these aren't legally binding. They keep putting reg negs in our statutes because they make us sit around the table and talk about actual regs with people who are going to have to work with these regs. So its great PR because members can now say they've really opened up the process for these people.[104]

While this ED official's comments better reflect the political forces that characterize the popularity of reg negs than do the comments of the OMB official, the ED official's comments are nonetheless misleading in so far as he spoke of the reg negs merely as "great PR." The attempt to allow interested publics to participate in the policymaking process is not an inconsequential function. It is central to what representatives are supposed to do.

A basic difference between the legislative veto and reg-neg mechanisms is that reg negs are clearly a more powerful solution to congressional policymaking needs than the legislative veto. Both were meant to enhance the power of members, and the interested groups they represent, to obtain information about proposed regulatory activities, to voice comments and objections about those activities, and to oversee their implementation. But the enactment of legislative veto shortcuts through constitutional procedure never fulfilled these functions.

Legislative vetoes might very well have served as prominent symbols of members' commitment to oversight, but it was the mandatory reporting requirements that worked to make ED's proposed activities more open to public view. While reg-neg provisions in ED statutes do not legally bind the department to any policy consensus that might emerge from the process, they require ED to invite representatives of the education community to discuss the potential implementation of individual regulations. These provisions address much more directly, and more powerfully, therefore, members' demand for openness in the regulatory process than did the legislative veto. Legal gimmicks that formally allow members to intrude on executive branch administrative powers seem to weaken rather than strengthen members' commitment to fulfilling their oversight responsibilities.

CONCLUSION

Exploring the consequences for educational policymaking of the legislative veto's invalidation provides empirical evidence that separation of powers procedures work to make members better at fulfilling their representative functions.[105] Hidden behind the Pell Grant policymaking authority delegated to the secretary of ED was a widespread bipartisan consensus among members that program funds should not be cut. By disturbing the structure of delegation in the Pell Grant statute—a statute containing a legislative veto provision that members had explicitly deemed a necessary congressional oversight tool—the Supreme Court's invalidation of the legislative veto jolted members into rescinding the secretary's authority and expressing their policy consensus in law.

Leaving the secretary's delegated authorities intact, free of legislative veto control, did not alter Pell Grant policy outcomes because members had always exercised control over these authorities through perfectly constitutional control mechanisms. But the Supreme Court's action established that the veto shortcut through constitutional procedure no longer symbolized congressional oversight power. Consequently, *Chadha* encouraged members to enact their policy convictions about the Pell Grant program into law. By upholding the constitutionally mandated procedures for legislative action, in other words, the Supreme Court made it easier for members to fulfill that aspect of their representative function that requires them to make Congress explicitly responsible for broadly supported public policies.

The Supreme Court's enforcement of separation of powers procedures also helped make members better at ensuring that their constituents would have opportunities to learn about and comment on proposed changes in regulatory policy. The legislative veto shortcut added no practical oversight value, in this regard, because the GEPA reporting requirements were already extremely successful in compelling consultation from the executive branch. The reg-neg substitute for the legislative veto, on the other hand, imposed the requirement on ED that it at least come face to face with those who stood to be affected by proposed regulations. Since the invalidation of the legislative veto focused members' attention on finding a new mechanism with which to exhibit their commitment to ensuring public access to the regulatory process—a mechanism that had to be more directly tied to members' actual objectives because symbolic constitutional shortcuts were no longer available—the legislative veto served members best by its absence.

Chapter Six

LEGISLATIVE VETOES OVER PRESIDENTIAL AUTHORITY TO EXTEND MOST-FAVORED-NATION STATUS

Among the most noteworthy of the legislative vetoes enacted in the foreign affairs area were those in the Jackson-Vanik amendment to the Trade Act of 1974, which imposed statutory restrictions on the president's authority to extend most-favored-nation (MFN) status to communist countries. Political scientists and legal scholars deemed these legislative vetoes powerful constitutional reforms indispensable to ensuring congressional participation in international trade policymaking. Yet, empirical analysis of the actual workings of these provisions show that in fact, legislative veto authority was inconsequential to congressional control of MFN policy. In addition, examination of the legislative veto at work shows that the Supreme Court's invalidation of the veto mechanism made members of Congress more attentive to their governing responsibilities. Together, these findings are highly instructive for understanding the separation of powers in practice.

THE SIGNIFICANCE OF THE JACKSON-VANIK VETO PROVISIONS

Those who believed that the legislative veto shortcut would alter the balance of policymaking powers between the branches have given special attention to the Jackson-Vanik veto provisions from the time of their enactment to the present. The provisions were enacted at a time of antagonistic interbranch relations. The Nixon administration hoped to use the Trade Bill of 1974 as a vehicle to advance its policy of détente with communist countries, but a variety of powerful forces within Congress stood firm against Nixon's attempt to pursue this objective.[1] Pro-labor groups opposed Nixon's trade bill because it threatened to make American workers more vulnerable to foreign trade competition.[2] Others objected to granting credit guarantees to the Soviets. They preferred to "allocate comparable funds to the development of American self-sufficiency in energy" than to assist the Soviets in bringing their natural resources to international markets.[3] All these groups allied themselves with Cold War liberals like Senator Henry Jackson (D-WA), who were intent on enacting statutory restrictions on the administration's authority to bestow trade benefits on communist countries.

By 1974, objections to Nixon's trade bill had translated into strong support for linking American foreign trade policy to human-rights issues. The catalyst that unified anti-administration forces behind this policy was the Soviet Union's decision to levy education repayment fees, in some cases running into tens of thousands of dollars, on any Soviet citizen emigrating to a non-communist country. In response, and with widespread congressional support, Senator Jackson and Rep. Charles Vanik (D-OH) introduced legislation prohibiting the extension of trade benefits to any communist country that placed restrictions on its citizens' right to emigrate.[4]

The administration, having already signed a bilateral trade agreement with the Soviet Union involving reciprocal extension of MFN status, vociferously objected to this potential linkage between emigration rights and international trade policy.[5] Claiming that such linkage would cause grave problems for American foreign policy, the administration threatened to veto the Jackson-Vanik amendment.[6]

To ensure enactment of his bill, Senator Jackson added provisions authorizing the president to waive the freedom of emigration restrictions. The final draft of the bill granted this authority on condition that the president provide "assurances" that such a waiver would substantially promote the freedom of emigration objectives of the Jackson-Vanik amendment.[7] The administration accepted this compromise because it knew that continuing congressional support for Jackson's amendment made deletion of the linkage provisions improbable, if not impossible.[8]

Members enacted legislative vetoes over this waiver authority because they feared it too vulnerable to presidential abuse. Were the president to exercise his waiver authority in favor of a country that members believed was not making enough progress in emigration rights, the legislative veto allowed them, simply by passing a disapproval resolution in either chamber, to prohibit the president from extending MFN status to that country.[9]

Members also enacted legislative vetoes over the president's authority to implement bilateral trade agreements. Without such agreements in place, the president could not initiate, nor extend, MFN status to potential trading partners. The legislative veto provisions prevented any such agreement from going into effect unless Congress explicitly approved the bilateral trade agreement by passing a resolution through both chambers.[10] As with the legislative veto provisions governing the president's waiver authority, members expressly demanded this legislative veto authority in order to ensure "close and continuing Congressional oversight of international trade negotiations and . . . implementation and operation of international trade agreements."[11]

Since the legislative veto was a "key aspect" of the delegation in Jackson-Vanik of policymaking powers to the president, members worried that the Supreme Court's invalidation of the mechanism would undermine Congress's capacity to supervise trade relations with communist countries.[12] Legal scholars explained that the invalidation of the Jackson-Vanik vetoes would "seriously hinder" congressional oversight capacity because "the President now may waive the ban on extension [of] MFN status without fear of a legislative veto. If the President does so, Congress must pass a bill forbidding the waiver in order to bar the extension of MFN status. Even then, the President may veto the bill." In the face of this significant change to the structure of delegation in Jackson-Vanik, these scholars predicted that Congress would enact new legislation to restore to itself some control.[13]

Those who called for such new legislation believed that the unconstitutional one-house disapproval vetoes governing the president's waiver authority should be amended to positive-approval forms of review.[14] The joint resolution of approval would comply with *Chadha* because it would pass both chambers as well as be presented to the president. And it would greatly strengthen Congress's hand since the president would be unable to take action unless Congress approved that action by joint resolution.

Those who opposed procedures that would require Congress to act affirmatively in each case argued that enacting new joint resolutions of approval in Jackson-Vanik would "reduce the flexibility of the executive branch to respond in a timely fashion to the requirements of foreign policy."[15] Senator Charles Grassley (R-IA) countered that "well, I don't know how else in a constitutional way to keep Congress involved in the MFN process the same way we have been under the potential of a congressional veto, which is no longer constitutional."[16] But Grassley failed to enact his joint resolution of approval, and Congress seemed doomed to losing control over presidential waivers of freedom of emigration restrictions.

Interbranch policy struggles under Jackson-Vanik in the late 1980s seemed to confirm the expectation that the loss of the legislative veto would alter the balance of power between the branches. The Tiananmen Square massacre of 1989 produced a powerful coalition within Congress that aimed to disapprove the presidential waiver of Jackson-Vanik restrictions necessary to continue extending MFN status to China.[17] In October 1990, this congressional coalition succeeded in passing through the House a resolution disapproving the president's waiver of freedom of emigration restrictions to China.[18] Had the *Chadha* Court upheld the constitutionality of the legislative veto, this resolution would have terminated MFN status for China.

But the successful passage of a disapproval resolution through the House in 1990 does not by itself prove that the legislative veto provisions in Jackson-Vanik had indeed been responsible for determining policy outcomes before *Chadha*. Proving or disproving such a conclusion requires empirical analysis of the interbranch dynamics of Jackson-Vanik policymaking, and of the actual role played by the legislative veto provisions in these policymaking processes.

CONGRESSIONAL OVERSIGHT UNDER JACKSON-VANIK

Implementing Jackson-Vanik

The Jackson-Vanik Amendment reflected members' drive to "recover some of the authority which had been ceded to the Executive in the area of foreign affairs."[19] Consequently, it became a lightning rod for critics who attacked Congress as incapable of dealing properly with the details of foreign policy. The Trade Act of 1974 was partly designed to take advantage of newly opened markets in Eastern Europe. But scholars who disapproved of the human-rights linkage in the Jackson-Vanik amendment predicted that trade would suffer because Eastern European nations would undoubtedly "forego economic advantages to avoid making changes in their internal domestic policies."[20] Critics warned that communist countries would "refuse to enter into commercial treaties even if they favored a liberal emigration policy, in order not to appear to be bending to the will of the U.S. Congress on a domestic matter."[21]

Critics of Jackson-Vanik cried "I told you so" when the Soviets rejected the U.S.-Soviet trade agreement that had been negotiated in 1972. Secretary of State Henry Kissinger blamed Congress for contributing to the Soviet rejection of the agreement because the Soviets had all along made very clear that they would not accept MFN status subject to political conditions.[22] Critics now had empirical evidence with which to castigate Congress for "poison[ing] the atmosphere for economic relations with the Soviet Union and other communist countries."[23] From this point of view, where the freedom of emigration restrictions appeared to have major consequences in international trade policy, the legislative vetoes poised to enforce these restrictions seemed of central importance to the policymaking process.

But the widespread view that Congress doomed U.S.-Soviet trade by legislatively linking it to emigration rights is historically inaccurate. Those who have taken the time to study the available evidence regarding Soviet conduct during May–December 1974 have found that the Soviets were, in fact, prepared to comply with Jackson-Vanik freedom of emigration standards.[24] The Soviets rejected the 1972 trade agreement not because of the Jackson-Vanik amendment to the Trade Act of 1974, but because of the passage of a different amendment to a different bill.[25]

The Stevenson amendment to the Export-Import Bank (Eximbank) Authorization Act of 1974 legislated a $300 million ceiling on loans or financial guarantees to the Soviet Union.[26] But access to Eximbank credits and investment guarantees was crucial to the Soviets. By October 1973, Eximbank had already extended half a billion dollars in credits to the Soviet Union, and estimates of credits to be extended in the future ran into billions of dollars.[27] The Soviets viewed these credits as "the principal means" for realizing their economic objectives, so the $300 million credit caps in the Stevenson amendment led them to reject the trade agreement.[28]

Since the Stevenson restrictions on credits were much more objectionable to the Soviets than the Jackson-Vanik freedom of emigration requirements, then it seems fair to ask why the Soviets did not object to the Stevenson amendment until after it was enacted, as they had to the Jackson-Vanik amendment. The reason was that the Nixon administration failed to inform them that the Stevenson amendment threatened to limit their access to Eximbank credits. Nixon administration officials seemed completely unaware that the amendment threatened to place an extremely severe limit on credits to the USSR.[29] Kissinger later admitted to his aides, in fact, "that he was not focusing on the [Stevenson] amendment when he should have."[30]

Only after the credit limitation was enacted did Kissinger order the State Department spokesman to denounce it as "grossly discriminatory."[31] Kissinger and his staff might have better tracked the bills affecting trade with communist countries if they had not been so focused on denouncing the legislative linkage of human rights and foreign policy. And critics of the legislative vetoes in Jackson-Vanik would have ceased citing the Soviet rejection of the trade agreement as evidence that the veto provisions were corrupting international trade policy.[32]

Once enacted, the freedom of emigration restrictions in Jackson-Vanik never proved central to interbranch policy disputes. The debates produced by the human-rights linkage in Jackson-Vanik revolved, instead, around the ambiguous objectives of the statute. This ambiguity lies in the disjunction between the statute's "general purpose" and the criteria it provides for evaluating progress toward this general purpose. The evaluation criteria are based exclusively on the "right or opportunity to emigrate."[33] The general purpose, however, is "to assure the continued dedication of the United States to fundamental human rights."[34] Consequently, even though the formative debates between Kissinger and Jackson over the human-rights linkage in Jackson-Vanik dealt specifically with emigration flows, human-rights groups have since argued that the statute "is concerned with the general issue of human rights as well as with the specific and articulated question of freedom of emigration. This interpretation is not only consistent with the language of the Act, but also with the universally accepted standards of human rights. Fundamental human rights cannot be narrowly restricted and confined to the right of emigration."[35]

From the start, the statutory ambiguity in Jackson-Vanik produced interbranch disagreements. The first time that the president chose to exercise his waiver authority was in 1976, when President Ford recommended an extension of MFN status to Romania. Ford addressed the emigration restrictions provisions directly, as required by law. His recommendation certified, Rep. Abner Mikva (D-IL) noted at hearings on the matter, that the extension of the waiver would "substantially promote the Trade Act's freedom of emigration objectives."[36] The president did not, however, address Romania's denial of political and religious rights to ethnic Hungarians in the Transylvania region of Romania. For this reason, Rep. Larry McDonald (D-GA) introduced a disapproval resolution in 1976—the first disapproval resolution introduced under the legislative veto authority in Jackson-Vanik—to overturn the president's waiver.[37]

But Ford successfully extended MFN to Romania in 1976 without much debate. In subsequent years, as the Romanian government engaged in increasingly egregious human-rights violations, debate over the scope of Jackson-Vanik became increasingly acrimonious. In a 1987 hearing on MFN status for Romania, Rep. Tom Lantos (D-CA) asserted that "it is a perversion of Jackson-Vanik if the [State] Department uses emigration figures as an index of how human rights are observed in a country."[38] But executive branch officials have consistently held, since Kissinger first agreed to the human-rights linkage in Jackson-Vanik, that the scope of the statute requires the president to address only freedom of emigration concerns.

At the May-June 1988 U.S.-Soviet summit meeting, for example, the Reagan administration went out of its way to raise the human-rights issue of emigration. Reminding Congress that "successive Administrations have opposed the extension of Jackson-Vanik criteria beyond emigration," State Department officials asserted that "this Administration continues to do so."[39] Had members enacted a mechanism in Jackson-Vanik authorizing them to shortcut constitutional procedure in order to formally broaden the scope of the statute's human-rights requirements, it might very well have become a major instrument of congressional policymaking power. Instead, the statute authorized them to shortcut constitutional procedure merely to enforce its freedom of emigration provisions.

Examination of how members exercised the oversight powers they enacted for themselves in Jackson-Vanik confirms that protecting freedom of emigration restrictions was never a significant congressional policy objective. Upon enacting the statute, members seemed intent on strictly enforcing the statute's "assurances" requirement. This forced the president to submit annual reports, or assurances, to Congress that countries receiving waivers of freedom of emigration restrictions would continue to improve their records in the future.[40] But when President Ford first waived the freedom of emigration restrictions for Romania, his assurances angered members because it consisted solely of the statement that both countries had agreed to "contribute to the solution of humanitarian problems on the basis of mutual confidence and good will."[41]

The House Ways and Means Committee complained that the president did "not specifically state that assurances have been received from the Romanian Government."[42] The Senate Finance Committee expressed "dissatisfaction with the text of the waiver . . . [which] merely makes vague reference to language concerning 'the solution of humanitarian problems on the basis of mutual confidence and goodwill.'"[43] Assistant Secretary of State Arthur Hartman explained, in testimony before Congress, that this vague presentation of assurances was necessary because of the sensitive nature of the trade negotiations.[44] Though Congress accepted these questionable assurances, the governing committees in both chambers made it clear that this approval should in no way be seen as a precedent for future reports that failed to present "assurances" in a substantive manner.[45]

Neither the president nor Congress itself, however, heeded this warning in subsequent waiver cases involving Hungary, Romania, and China. In these cases, Congress interpreted the assurances requirement much more "broadly," without insistence on "specific or formal assurances of future liberalization of emigration policy."[46] Congress reserved its insistence for that part of the review procedure that required the president to report and consult annually over every extension of MFN status to a communist country. The quality of the assurances was inconsequential because members were not particularly concerned about enforcing the freedom of emigration restrictions. The annual review process tied to the assurances requirement, on the other hand, was part of the "vital role of Congress" in the making of international trade policy.[47] Tracing the actual workings of the legislative vetoes governing the president's Jackson-Vanik authorities makes it possible to understand how members themselves defined this role.

LEGISLATIVE VETOES IN ACTION

Jackson-Vanik contains three sets of legislative veto provisions intended to protect and enhance congressional policymaking power. These include the provisions placed over the president's authority to waive Jackson-Vanik restrictions, those governing the approval of bilateral trade agreements, and the provisions authorizing either chamber to overturn a presidential determination that a communist country should no longer be subject to Jackson-Vanik. Exploration of the workings of these provisions both demonstrates that the legislative veto mechanism was irrelevant to congressional policymaking control and also points to those procedures that made congressional control over policy outcomes possible.

Presidential Waiver Authority

The legislative veto governing the president's authority to extend twelve-month waivers of the Jackson-Vanik freedom of emigration restrictions authorized members to overturn any such waiver by passing a one-house disapproval resolution. Though such resolutions were introduced in every Congress since 1976, when the president first exercised his authority to extend a Jackson-Vanik waiver, none of these resolutions ever received positive action from the relevant committees.[48] In the one instance when such a resolution was brought to a vote on the floor of either chamber, Rep. Richard Schulze's (R-PA) attempt to disapprove the president's waiver for Romania in 1979, the resolution was defeated by a large margin.[49] Serious congressional attempts to overturn presidential waivers did not take the form of disapproval resolutions, that is, legislative vetoes. Such attempts consisted, rather, of bills, known as "conditions bills," that were independent of the congressional review process built into the waiver authority in Jackson-Vanik.

A key difference between Jackson-Vanik disapproval resolutions and their significantly more powerful relatives is that conditions bills allowed Congress to threaten the president's waiver on whatever grounds members deemed appropriate. Disapproval resolutions ostensibly became necessary only if Congress objected to the president's waiver of the statute's freedom of emigration requirements. But conditions bills were independent of the Jackson-Vanik statute. The cases in which Congress came closest to overturning the president's waiver of Jackson-Vanik restrictions demonstrate how this independence led conditions bills to become the central procedural vehicle for congressional control of MFN policy under the statute.

The first serious congressional threat to overturn the president's extension of MFN occurred in 1987 with respect to Romania. Anti-Romanian sentiment became widespread in Congress in the mid- to late-1980s in response to markedly worsening human-rights conditions there. By introducing bills threatening to suspend Romania's MFN status, members were able to make specific reference to the Romanian government's persecution of religious and ethnic minorities. "While Jackson-Vanik uses the specific right of free emigration by which to measure progress in human rights," stated Senator Bill Armstrong (R-CO), a co-sponsor of the conditions bill, "it would be negligent to ignore Romania's human rights abuses in other areas. This is particularly true in light of the fact that the United States Helsinki Watch Committee, among others, has called the Romanian Government 'one of the most egregious offenders of human rights in Eastern Europe.'"[50]

Critics of these bills objected to broadening the human-rights linkage in MFN policy. Senator Bob Packwood (R-OR), for example, explained that "the conduct of Romania, when it comes to religious freedom, is brutish, boorish, deplorable, disgusting. There is no question about that. But the Jackson-Vanik amendment and the extension of most-favored-nation status to Romania is premised on emigration; emigration, not religious freedom. Romania has a better record of emigration than any other European Eastern bloc country."[51]

The bills conditioning MFN for Romania were ultimately moot because the Ceauşescu regime itself rejected MFN before Congress had the opportunity to suspend it. Trade journals reported that "Romania, which renounced its waiver before the question of renewal for 1988 came up, would have lost the waiver anyway because of human rights concerns unrelated to emigration."[52] Though the conditions bills had yet to be enacted, the Romanian government considered them "an inadmissible interference in Romania's domestic affairs, unrelated with the commercial ties between Romania and the United States of

America."[53] A State Department official from the Romania desk explained that once Deputy Secretary of State John Whitehead went to Romania in 1987 to "read them the riot act on human-rights abuses," and to make it clear to Romanian officials that the Reagan administration would not "go to bat for them in Congress" unless they improved their human-rights record, the Romanian government "decided to pull out."[54]

Though Armstrong never succeeded in enacting his bill into law, he and his co-sponsors believed they had won an important victory. Both the House and the Senate passed bills that threatened to suspend MFN for Romania unless the president certified that the Romanian government would improve its treatment of ethnic and religious minorities. Such a broad linkage of human rights to foreign policymaking had never received such widespread support.[55]

An even more contentious case in which Congress threatened to overturn the president's waiver involved China in 1990. Congressional attempts to punish China for the Tiananmen Square massacre in 1989 were very similar to those involving Romania a few years earlier. In both cases, members fought the president's decision to extend the Jackson-Vanik waiver by introducing conditions bills that specified the human-rights violations at issue rather than pushing for disapproval resolutions pursuant to Jackson-Vanik.[56] One of the supporters of the bill conditioning the president's extension of MFN to China made specific reference to the 1987 bill conditioning Romania's MFN, noting that "while Jackson-Vanik specifically focuses on emigration figures, the level of compliance with internationally recognized human rights standards must be included in our criteria. I think part of the precedence for that was our work in the mid-1980's on suspending and then perhaps even revoking MFN for Romania."[57] Opposition to the conditions bills in the China case, as in the Romania case, was based on the view that Jackson-Vanik should not be distorted by expansive readings.[58]

In contrast to the Romanian case, members had full legal access to the disapproval resolution procedure by the time President Bush proposed a waiver of Jackson-Vanik restrictions for China in 1990. The legal status of the procedure was not so clear between 1983, when the Supreme Court invalidated the legislative veto mechanism in *Chadha,* and 1990, when Congress enacted the procedural changes to Jackson-Vanik required by the legal reasoning in *Chadha.*[59] Conditions bills nonetheless continued to serve as the lightning rod for interbranch tension after Congress fixed the unconstitutional defect in the disapproval resolution procedure.

"In the Congressional context, we have one of two options," Rep. Stephen Solarz (D-NY) explained with respect to procedural mechanisms for attacking the president's extension of MFN to China: "We can either move on a resolution of disapproval, which rejects the President's determination. Or we can adopt legislation which would establish conditions, in addition to freedom of emigration, that China would have to meet in order for MFN to be renewed when it came up for a subsequent determination a year from now."[60] The first option, terminating MFN status with a resolution disapproving the president's waiver, did not provide members the opportunity to express their concerns over China's human-rights violations, nor did it allow them to set guidelines by which China could satisfy their concerns. So Solarz introduced a bill, with several co-sponsors, that would require the president to certify that China had released political prisoners. The bill also required the Chinese government to "provide the names of and account fully for the several hundred people it says were arrested in last year's crackdown and since released."[61] Solarz's conditions bill, unlike the disapproval resolutions threatening to overturn the president's waiver, received immediate and widespread support in Congress.[62]

The need to expand the scope of the human-rights linkage in Jackson-Vanik might have been the most important factor in triggering the use of conditions bills. But there was nothing in the Jackson-Vanik disapproval resolution procedure that prevented Congress from overturning presidential waivers for reasons completely unrelated to freedom of emigration restrictions. Congress never used the Jackson-Vanik vetoes to exact particular policy outcomes from the president because the vetoes represented a policy outcome, outright denial of MFN, that members had no interest in achieving. Unlike conditions bills, disapproval resolutions did not allow Congress to specify when, why, how, and for how long the president should suspend MFN. Conditions bills served as the central procedural mechanism for congressional exercise of control over policymaking, therefore, because they were "more feasible politically than an outright ban."[63] And precisely because they were more feasible, conditions bills gave Congress more power with which to compel on-going consultation from the president.

In describing how sponsors of the 1987 bill conditioning MFN for Romania acquired support from their colleagues, one of the congressional staff members who worked on the bill explained that most members found actual termination of MFN too draconian. The first time her office introduced a conditions bill rather than a disapproval resolution to "kill MFN for Romania," in 1985, it did not receive much support from members: "It was essentially the same as the disapproval resolutions Phil Crane had been introducing for years and years except that our bill talked about rights of ethnic minorities and religious rights."[64] When they reintroduced the bill in 1987, however, they "had a much more sophisticated bill" that threatened to "suspend" rather than "terminate" Romania's MFN status for six months instead of one year. Rep. Frank Wolf (R-VA) introduced the bill by drawing attention to its "sophisticated" qualities: "[Our last] amendment on this floor . . . would have totally [terminated MFN for Romania.] This one will suspend for 6 months and is totally different."[65] To object to this bill, critics claimed that its effect would be just as draconian as enacting a disapproval resolution: "All witnesses from the business community involved in trade with Romania were in agreement with the administration that a 6 month suspension would have the same effect as letting MFN status lapse altogether. In the everyday world of business decisions it is not conceivable that trade, interrupted for 6 months—would easily resume again."[66]

Though less explicit, congressional opposition to outright bans on MFN status was equally strong in policy toward China after the Tiananmen Square massacre. Members introduced several different conditions bills affecting MFN status for China. But the most successful were those that postponed actual suspension of MFN for the longest period of time, or attached the weakest conditions to the president's waiver authority. In 1990, for example, the House Ways and Means Committee adopted Rep. Donald Pease's (D-OH) bill which would have required President Bush to certify before 4 June 1991 that China had made "significant progress" toward achieving specific human-rights goals.[67] In adopting Pease's bill, the committee rejected a tougher substitute offered by Rep. Thomas Downey (D-NY). Like Pease's bill, Downey's would have allowed the president's 1990 waiver to stand. But it would have required the Chinese to meet—not merely make progress toward—specified standards of behavior by the following June.[68]

Unlike disapproval resolutions, which would terminate MFN status upon enactment, the conditions bills would have given China a full year to demonstrate that it was making some sort of progress in a number of human-rights areas before denying it MFN status. Furthermore, determination of whether or not China had made sufficient progress would rest with the president. One of the sponsors of a conditions bill noted explicitly that he and his supporters "had no intention of 'painting President Bush into a corner': We sought to fashion conditions that would prove effective and meaningful in the struggle for better human rights policy in China without being so stringent that the Government of the People's Republic of China would not be able to fully comply within the allotted time period and our President would be forced to cut off MFN."[69] All of these conditions bills allowed the president more time and more negotiating leeway than the disapproval resolution, introduced pursuant to the legislative veto provision in Jackson-Vanik, which threatened to "cancel China's current MFN eligibility outright."[70]

Even the strongest supporters of disapproval resolutions believed that actual, outright termination of MFN status was not a policy outcome for which there would ever be much support. In fact, many of them argued that disapproval resolutions were never really meant to achieve such an outcome. In calling for support of his resolution disapproving MFN for Romania in 1986, for example, Rep. Tony Hall (D-OH) argued that "discharging and passing this resolution will not end MFN for Romania. That would require action by both bodies and a signature from the President. [But a strong vote on] this resolution . . . will send a strong signal to the Romanian Government that there is deep congressional concern about human rights violations and repression in Romania."[71] One of the staffers of a leading proponent of disapproval resolutions explained, similarly, that "we don't actually want to see our disapproval resolutions pass, of course. No one wants to. The ideal, as we see it, is to get strong votes in the House and Senate approving the resolution, and then get the president to veto it. This is the best way to send a definitive, strong message to the Chinese that they're on wobbly ground."[72]

By virtue of their greater popularity among members, however, conditions bills proved a much more powerful mechanism than disapproval resolutions by which to send a message protesting human-rights abuses. "Conditionality is more threatening to Beijing than the disapproval resolutions," one congressional staff member explained, because

> it gets a lot more support in Congress. Disapproval resolutions don't really catch Beijing's attention as much because not as many people vote for them. Besides, they represent a sledgehammer policy. If we really do terminate MFN, then Beijing would probably say, "Okay, fine. Go right ahead. Just don't tell us what to do with our own people." Conditions bills, on the other hand, keep us involved so Beijing can't so easily say, "Okay, fine, we'll just do as we please."[73]

To show the threatening power of conditions bills, Rep. Pease noted that "the mere introduction" of his conditions bill "resulted in the release of a number of political prisoners in China."[74]

Most members opposed outright termination of MFN for three reasons. First, it was clear to them that threats that actually resulted in the termination of MFN would hurt American businesses. The 1987 conditions bill threatening Romanian MFN received widespread support in part because the economic situation in Romania was so weak that very few American businesses cared about extending MFN to Romania for another year.[75] In the China case, in contrast, the Bush administration made sure to note that "denying MFN status to China . . . would also have extremely damaging economic consequences for U.S. business and U.S. consumers."[76]

The second reason why terminating MFN has been an unpopular policy option is that it has been considered counterproductive with respect to achieving human-rights goals. Former ambassador to China Winston Lord warned, for example, that immediate "termination of the trade status would hurt the wrong people in China."[77] And David Michael Lampton, the president of the National Committee on U.S.-China Relations, argued that "Congress should take into account the desires of the Chinese people. Citizens of the PRC with whom I have spoken, in circumstances where I believe I heard their deeply felt convictions, do not want MFN treatment for China ended. These are persons who have no sympathy for Beijing's current policy. Indeed, they have suffered under it."[78] One of the congressional staff members responsible for meeting with interested groups on the issue noted that "student groups themselves, by the way—the groups that have been most vocal on the anti-China side, that is—did not want to cut off MFN with disapproval resolutions right away."[79]

The third reason why ending MFN has never been a policy that has received much congressional support is that it seemed to carry with it the possibility of opening an unseemly can of worms for American human-rights policy. To terminate the MFN status of a communist country because of human-rights violations would bring into question the MFN status of a whole set of countries that were not subject to the Jackson-Vanik statute.[80] "Among the countries that have most-favored-nation status today," noted Senator Packwood in objecting to those intent on punishing China by removing its MFN status, "are Libya, Iran, Iraq, Syria, all bastions of democracy and protectors of civil liberties. Nonsense."[81] In sum, conditions bills received wider support among members than disapproval resolutions because the immediate revocation of MFN status that would result from the enactment of a disapproval resolution was not a viable policy option.

The MFN status of the Soviet Union during the first two decades of Jackson-Vanik's history seems to present a counter-example to the view that disapproval resolutions never represented a viable policy option. Had the president had occasion to ask for annual waivers of Jackson-Vanik restrictions for the Soviet Union, Congress might very well have chosen MFN termination as a policy option. In the case of the Soviet Union, there was widespread support for denying MFN status completely. When, during a period of increased emigration in 1978–79, the Carter administration suggested that it grant a one-year waiver of Jackson-Vanik to the Soviet Union, Senator Jackson insisted that the high emigration rate did not justify granting MFN status. The Soviet Union had provided the impetus for the Jackson-Vanik restrictions, after all, and remained the amendment's principal target.[82]

Sensitive to the significance of the Soviet case, the Bush administration loosened Jackson-Vanik restrictions on the Soviet Union much more slowly than on any other country emerging from communism. By 1989, when more than sixty thousand Jewish emigrants left the Soviet Union, it was clear that Gorbachev's administration had removed emigration restraints on Jews and other ethnic and religious minorities. Nonetheless, the administration chose not to extend MFN to the Soviet Union because freedom of emigration had not yet been codified in Soviet law, a condition that went beyond the Jackson-Vanik requirements.[83]

But the particularly high Jackson-Vanik standards to which the Soviet Union was held does not show that members would have gladly vetoed presidential waivers of Jackson-Vanik restrictions if they had

had an opportunity to do so. The denial of MFN for the Soviet Union was a viable policy option because it represented the status quo. One congressional staff member responsible for Jackson-Vanik issues elaborated on the significance of the status quo for MFN policy by noting that, in the case of the Soviet Union, "There's no rug in place for Congress to pull out from under business's feet. There's no business lobby that can come up here and say things like, 'well the reason we invested in China in 1982 is that we had just completed a trade agreement, and now you're going to take it away from us?' There's no such constituency for the USSR."[84] Had the Soviet Union been granted MFN in 1974, thereby becoming subject to the legislative vetoes governing the president's annual waiver authority, it is unlikely that the vetoes would have been any more significant in interbranch struggles over MFN policy toward the Soviet Union than they were with respect to other communist countries.

Thus, though the legislative vetoes governing the president's waiver authority never carried policymaking power, the annual review procedure tied to these vetoes proved essential to congressional oversight of MFN policy. By forcing the president to report proposed Jackson-Vanik waivers annually to Congress, and by providing members with the opportunity to express their opinions about any such waivers, the Jackson-Vanik review process, explained a USTR official, has served as "the key to congressional leverage."[85] It has provided members with leverage over the president's decisions by ensuring expedited, or "fast-track," procedures for resolutions intended to overturn Jackson-Vanik waivers.[84] By imposing time limits on committee and floor action as well as severe restrictions on any amendments, fast-track procedures guarantee that members' formal objections to presidential waivers will be put to a vote. With such a guarantee, members have been able to demand that the president pay attention to their concerns.[87]

For example, when President Bush proposed an extension of MFN for China in 1991, members expressed more widespread support for bills conditioning the president's waiver than they ever had before in the history of Jackson-Vanik.[88] In response, President Bush wrote a detailed letter outlining the various ways in which his administration planned to push the Chinese government into complying with members' human-rights demands.[89] Satisfied that the president had incorporated their demands into his policy toward China, members who were eager to punish China but were unsure about the wisdom of imposing legal demands on the Chinese government finally agreed to withdraw their support for bills conditioning the president's authority.

The presence of legislative veto authority actually weakened the power of the Jackson-Vanik annual review procedure to serve members' oversight goals. With such a shortcut in place, members could not use disapproval resolutions to express their opinions about proposed presidential extensions of MFN. A simple majority in one chamber voting in favor of such a resolution would have required actual termination of MFN. By enforcing the constitutional requirement that disapproval resolutions pass both chambers and be presented to the president, the Supreme Court's invalidation of the legislative veto made it possible for a larger number of members to vote in favor of resolutions disapproving presidential waivers without worrying that their votes would result in outright revocation of MFN. Not until after members amended Jackson-Vanik to comply with *Chadha,* therefore, did a majority of either chamber vote in favor of a Jackson-Vanik disapproval resolution.[90]

The resolution that threatened China's MFN status in 1990 succeeded in the House precisely because members knew that it would mean nothing, legally, without joint Senate approval. And they knew that Senate approval was impossible since the House resolution was not passed until the very end of the congressional session, leaving no time for the Senate to approve a similar resolution. Supporters of the resolution explained that its success in the House "was a more symbolic than substantive act."[91] The presence of legislative veto authority would have made such a symbolic act impossible.

Approval of Bilateral Trade Agreements

The legislative vetoes governing the president's authority to enter into bilateral trade agreements with communist countries required that Congress approve such agreements by passing an approval resolution through both chambers.[92] Between the time this review procedure was enacted in 1974 and tainted by the Supreme Court's invalidation of the legislative veto in 1983, Congress passed without controversy the necessary approval resolutions for every trade agreement submitted by the president.[93] After 1983, it was not clear whether the review procedure remained binding on the president. If it was deemed not binding, or severable from the president's authority to negotiate bilateral trade agreements, then "the President might enter into such an agreement and proclaim MFN for the country concerned without seeking Congressional approval. This could extinguish the role of Congress in approval of such trade agreements."[94] In 1989, when the Bush administration tentatively began to negotiate a trade agreement with the Soviet Union, the legal uncertainties surrounding the approval resolution procedure in Jackson-Vanik threatened to have serious political consequences.

The possible severability of the legislative veto provision from the president's authority to negotiate bilateral trade agreements presented the Bush administration with two options. "We could either tough it out" by negotiating and implementing a trade agreement with the Soviet Union without submitting it to Congress for approval, explained one member of the White House Counsel's Office who participated in the inter-agency policy group formed to decide how to proceed. "Or we could work with Congress" to amend Jackson-Vanik into compliance with *Chadha*, thereby eliminating legal uncertainties, "and then proceed as usual in submitting the agreement for congressional approval." The "downsides to option one," he explained, were twofold: "If we proceeded on the assumption that we could implement a bilateral agreement without congressional approval, some private party might take it to court, arguing that the concurrent resolutions were not severable, and that would slow down the process for months. More importantly, Congress would undoubtedly get angry and rescind the authority altogether."[95] The "downside to option two" was that "Congress might not be able to enact the required amendments to the statute in time. All of us, knowing that Jackson-Vanik is a sacred cow up on the Hill, were afraid that anything to do with Jackson-Vanik and the Soviet Union would be incredibly controversial and that it would take forever to get anything done."[96]

When members got wind that an inter-agency policy group was discussing these various options, the Bush administration's best course of action quickly became self-evident. A State Department official who had participated in the policy group recalled that "Rostie and Bentsen" (Rep. Daniel Rostenkowski [D-IL] and Senator Lloyd Bentsen [D-TX], the respective chairs of the committees responsible for Trade Act issues, the House Ways and Means Committee and Senate Finance Committee) "made it very clear that it was not a good idea for us to even think about signing a binding trade agreement with the Soviet Union without submitting it to Congress." Even though administration officials believed that the legally tainted review process was severable from Jackson-Vanik, and that the administration could therefore "engage in a binding agreement without Congress if we really wanted to," they also believed that "it would be politically stupid to try to behave that way."[97]

The USTR official in the group explained, similarly, "We all figured out pretty quickly that Congress could have amended the statute to rescind our authority in a second, if we made it easy for them by bullying them around."[98] The administration encouraged Congress to amend Jackson-Vanik, therefore, to make the bilateral trade agreement approval process comply with *Chadha*. Members did so in 1990 with a simple technical change that required Congress to present its approval resolutions to the president before they could take effect.[99]

The Supreme Court's invalidation of the legislative veto made it legally feasible for the administration to consider implementing a new Soviet trade agreement without congressional approval. The administration found it politically infeasible to take advantage of its newly acquired powers, however, because members were intent on protecting their opportunity to review proposed treaties. Were the administration to have seriously threatened this opportunity for congressional review, members would have rescinded the president's negotiating authority altogether. It was not the legislative veto shortcut itself but the congressional review authority in Jackson-Vanik that members were poised to spring into action in order to protect with their lawmaking power.

Exemption from Jackson-Vanik Requirements

The president's authority to exempt communist countries from Jackson-Vanik freedom of emigration requirements was subject to a veto provision that authorized either chamber to overturn the president's exemption by passing a disapproval resolution.[100] This provision was "cured" of its constitutional infirmities in 1990 by amendments requiring a joint resolution rather than a one-house veto to overturn the president's exemptions.[101] No president ever asked for such an exemption, however, until after the collapse of the communist bloc. In response to the first attempt to use this authority, when President Bush certified in 1990 that Hungary was in compliance with all Jackson-Vanik requirements, members accepted the president's exemption without question.[102] In addition, they permanently exempted Hungary and Czechoslovakia from Jackson-Vanik restrictions, thereby eliminating the need for annual waivers.[103]

The president's authority to deem countries in compliance with Jackson-Vanik restrictions was rarely the occasion for any political action or even proposed political action, let alone for any interbranch power struggles. As such, the legislative vetoes governing it were irrelevant to congressional control over policy outcomes under Jackson-Vanik.

CONCLUSION: POLICYMAKING GOALS AND THE SEPARATION OF POWERS

Analysis of the interbranch power struggles associated with the evolution of MFN policymaking under Jackson-Vanik clarifies the different objectives pursued by executive branch officials and members of Congress. Executive branch officials have fought to prevent all congressional attempts to veto or impose any legal conditions on the president's policy decisions. An attorney from the State Department Legal Adviser's Office explained that all administrations have felt responsible for protecting the presidency from formal legal constraints on its foreign policymaking authority. This has been particularly acute in the case of Jackson-Vanik, he explained further, because MFN is a much more effective negotiating tool when used in an informal rather than a formal way: "Of course the president uses the threat of MFN removal to fight for human-rights issues. And, of course, he does this partly because Congress demands it of him. But the administration can much more effectively bring pressure to bear on human-rights issues when it does it by quiet, behind-the-scenes diplomacy than when it is required by statute."[104]

Executive branch officials viewed existing Jackson-Vanik review requirements as useful to the president's "quiet, behind-the-scenes diplomacy"—as long as they never resulted in legal directives. "Having a threat that the president can blame on Congress strengthens the president's hand."[105] Since 1974, executive branch officials have been suc-

111

cessful at ensuring that all disapproval resolutions and conditions bills remained no more than serious threats.[106]

Though members never succeeded in imposing new legal constraints on the president's negotiating authorities, they made sure to force executive branch officials to make congressional concerns central to the policymaking process. Every administration since 1974 has argued that Jackson-Vanik review procedures were only relevant to freedom of emigration issues, but members of Congress succeeded in broadening the human-rights concerns affecting MFN policy. Executive branch officials who testified on the president's waivers for Romania and China spent more time discussing the rights of religious minorities, abuse of political prisoners, and trade problems than emigration statistics. In the China case, the administration justified its waiver of Jackson-Vanik restrictions partly on the grounds that "MFN would advance . . . the cause of human rights and reform in China."[107] President Bush explained that "we clearly share the same goals. We want to see China return to the path of reform, show greater respect for human rights, adhere to international norms on weapons sales, and practice fair trade."[108]

Similarly, human-rights violations completely unrelated to freedom of emigration led the administration to postpone its request for a Jackson-Vanik waiver for Romania in 1989. The administration contemplated extending MFN to Romania as soon as the Ceauşescu regime was toppled, but as a staffer of a member who had dedicated himself to expanding the scope of Jackson-Vanik human-rights concerns explained,

> Ceauşescu was ousted in December 1989 and things were looking good for re-extending MFN to Romania, but then in June 1990, the group in power started killing protesters, so the administration decided not to ask for MFN then. Ambassador Allan "Thumpy" Green happened to be scheduled to come over to meet with us when all of this happened. "I was coming to tell you that we would ask for MFN for Romania, and that you should support the State Department on this, but with the news this morning, I'm here to say that now is not the time to give Romania MFN." So they didn't ask for it then.[109]

One of the officers at the Romania desk of the Commerce Department confirmed this explanation of the administration's decision to postpone extension of MFN for Romania, concluding that "there's no question that within the administration, MFN is tied to political problems much broader than just emigration rights."[110]

Members were able to force open the Jackson-Vanik linkage into a broad concern for human rights by demanding regular communication between the branches. Administrations were able to resist legal directives from Congress, likewise, by complying with demands for communication. In 1991, for example, a threateningly high number of powerful members supported the bill conditioning the president's extension of MFN to China. These members promised not to vote for the bill when the administration addressed their concerns directly during the annual review period. Senator Max Baucus (D-MT) explained that:

> this is an issue where we all share common goals—to bring about reform in China while maintaining trade with the world's largest nation. . . . That is why I and several of my colleagues have put pressure on the administration to take action at stopping abuses by China. Late last week, President Bush wrote me a lengthy letter. It was not—as some have said—filled with "mostly rhetoric." It was, for the first time in this administration, a comprehensive review of our policy toward China and a plan for future relations.[111]

Members promised not to support bills conditioning the president's authority because they were guaranteed constant, albeit informal, executive branch consultation and attention in return.

Part of the informal price paid by the Bush administration in its "fierce political battle . . . to win the renewal of China's most-favored-nation trade status" included a wide-ranging investigation of unfair discrimination by China against American products.[112] It also included deference to congressional leaders in determining the priorities in Secretary of State Baker's agenda for meeting with Chinese leaders in November 1991. Baker opened his talks with "a series of specific requests that China cease any transfers of nuclear weapons technology to countries like Algeria and Iran and that it release some of the pro-democracy political prisoners."[113] These concerns had fueled congressional attempts to condition China's MFN status. Consequently, members were reluctant to criticize the Baker mission when he returned with only limited commitments from Chinese leaders "because of a sense that he had pressed the Chinese for change in the areas that Congress was most concerned about."[114]

As executive branch officials fought to protect legal discretion for the presidency, members of Congress strove to obtain regular information about proposed policies as well as attention to their opinions on those policies. In the midst of this interbranch dynamic, the legislative veto shortcut proved inconsequential to the balance of policymaking power between the branches. Those who have thought otherwise have been insensitive to the difference between conditions bills and disapproval resolutions—legislative veto provisions authorized the disapproval resolution procedure, but it was with conditions bills that members succeeded in demanding attention from the president to their broad human-rights concerns. In addition, when members quietly threatened to rescind the president's authority to negotiate bilateral trade agreements, they were not threatening retaliation against loss of the veto provision in the statute, but against the possibility of losing their opportunity to review proposed agreements.

Though the legislative veto did not play a significant role in determining policy outcomes, the Supreme Court's invalidation of the mechanism nonetheless affected the ways in which members pursued their objectives. *Chadha* was probably partly responsible for focusing members' creative energies on demanding informal policy concessions from the president.[115] It was not until after the Supreme Court invalidated the legislative veto that members began threatening to condition the president's waivers with new legal demands apart from freedom of emigration requirements. It was not until after *Chadha* that a bill threatened to apply these new legal demands after a trial period in which the president was given time to certify that certain progress had been made.[116] It was not until after members were forced to search for alternatives to the disapproval resolution procedure, in other words, that they began to introduce conditions bills as tools for participating in the president's decisions about trade negotiations with communist countries.

According to one State Department official, conditions bills would have become the main mechanism for congressional policymaking under Jackson-Vanik irrespective of the presence or absence of legislative veto authority. "The reason you first start getting conditions bills in 1985," he explained, "is that there was no occasion for using them before that."[117] Whether the egregious human-rights violations in Romania and China were in fact solely responsible for leading members to adopt conditions bills is not entirely clear. It is fair to say, however, that the Supreme Court's invalidation of the legislative veto helped speed up the process by which members discovered the power of conditions bills to force the president to pay attention and respond to congressional views. It is certainly true, furthermore, that the Supreme Court's invalidation of the mechanism made it less consequential, and thus easier, for members to use the disapproval resolution procedure to voice their opinions. By restoring separation of powers procedures, therefore, the Supreme Court led members to focus more intently on the very policymaking objectives they had been pursuing since Jackson-Vanik was first enacted.

Chapter Seven
CONCLUSION

On 26 June 1995, in a front-page obituary tribute to former Chief
Justice Warren Burger, the *New York Times* said of Burger's landmark
Chadha decision that it "altered the balance of power between the
executive and legislative branches."[1] Thus did the nation's newspaper
of record testify to the persistence of the common wisdom that the
legislative veto had been a powerful instrument of congressional oversight. However, as the preceding case studies have shown, the common wisdom does not withstand scrutiny.

On the contrary, the case studies throw into sharp relief three characteristics of the legislative veto at work. First, even with legislative
veto authority available, members exercised control over policy outcomes in ways that were perfectly constitutional. Members did not
need the legislative veto shortcut to force executive branch officials to
attend to congressional concerns, because the most useful sources of
congressional oversight power—the power to make laws, and the
power to require that executive branch and independent agency officials report proposed actions before implementation—are well nestled
in the authorities granted to members by Article I of the Constitution.
Accordingly, to achieve their Pell Grant policy objectives, members
enacted the necessary needs analysis formula into law when they disapproved of the formula promulgated by the Department of Education. To prohibit Secretary of Education William Bennett, one of the

Reagan administration's leading "Congress bashers," from implementing proposed regulations that members' constituents found objectionable, members made good use of the extensive reporting and waiting requirements they had enacted into the General Education Provisions Act (GEPA).

Similarly, to prevent the Federal Trade Commission of the 1970s, the quintessential "runaway" agency, from implementing controversial regulatory policies, members demanded that the FTC's rulemaking activities be open to the participation of potentially affected groups. Members also subjected the agency's rules to broad judicial review. And to ensure that the president linked human-rights issues to extensions of trade opportunities for communist countries, members annually threatened to enact laws circumscribing his negotiating authority.

Long before the Supreme Court invalidated the legislative veto shortcut, executive branch officials understood that the real sources of congressional policymaking power lay elsewhere and were perfectly constitutional. So they knew better than to try to turn the Supreme Court's decision into a legal mandate for thwarting congressional policy objectives. Bush administration officials chose to continue abiding by the congressional approval procedure required for bilateral trade agreements, therefore, even though they believed that the Supreme Court's *Chadha* decision had legally freed them to ignore it. Had they chosen to ignore the approval requirement, they would have provoked Congress to exercise its lawmaking power to impose new legal restrictions on the president's authority to negotiate international trade agreements.

Unlike these Bush officials, William Bennett attempted to take advantage of his newfound legal authority, after *Chadha,* to ignore congressional concerns. He implemented a set of regulations on student data verification that flew in the face of widespread congressional objections. But it did not take long for his defiance of Congress to turn into a pyrrhic victory. Congress "legislated over" his controversial regulations with a set of new regulations that better reflected members' policy views.

Second, in addition to showing Congress's formidable oversight powers at work, the case studies also demonstrate that members never found the legislative veto shortcut useful for achieving their desired policy outcomes. When executive branch actions clearly violated bipartisan congressional expectations, members responded swiftly and emphatically by enacting, or making credible threats to enact, new law. And in the more common situation in which members either were not certain as to the best way of implementing a particular policy, or had specific opinions that would not easily be supported by a majority of their colleagues, they preferred to participate informally in policy implementation through report-and-wait provisions rather than the legislative veto.

The enactment of legislative veto provisions did indeed suggest that members were trying to change constitutional arrangements in order to turn themselves into full-time administrators of executive powers. But in practice, members were actually not interested in pursuing such rearrangements of power. The legislative veto was unlikely ever to have much policymaking relevance because members relied on and took advantage of their institutional separation from final implementation decisions.

Thus, the legislative veto in the Trade Act proved inconsequential to policy outcomes because it enabled Congress to evade the president's veto power, thereby making it easier for members to terminate most-favored-nation status to communist countries. But members did not want to force the president to implement such a policy. Though their rhetoric, fueled by sweeping disgust for China's Tiananmen Square massacre, demanded such termination, members chose to leave final policymaking authority in the presidency because they knew that outright termination of MFN was certain to hurt American businesses. It was also more likely to worsen human-rights conditions than to achieve the intended improvements.

The legislative veto provisions governing the regulatory activities of the Department of Education tell a similar story. In GEPA, the unconstitutional provisions authorized members to overturn proposed rules through one-house disapproval resolutions. But members had less interest in overturning proposed rules than they had in compelling consultation from the administration on the substance of these proposed rules. And members were perfectly able to compel such consultation by relying on the extensive reporting requirements in the statute.

While members avoided making themselves individually accountable for the actual implementation of policy, they were eager to take responsibility for ensuring ongoing consultation from the executive branch on administrative processes. Members demand openness in executive branch and independent agency activities because it provides them and their constituents with advance warning of potentially controversial actions about which they would want to make sure to comment.

Moreover, members' capacity to compel consultation on proposed policies can be used to serve different policymaking objectives. In the case of the Trade Act, members sought to voice their strong opinions in a way that would protect the discretion of executive branch officials to determine policy outcomes. In the case of GEPA, extensive reporting requirements enabled members to prevent the Reagan and Bush administrations from imposing major changes to existing regulatory policies. And in the case of the FTC, openness in the regulatory process enabled Congress to begin forcing a reversal in the agency's controversial policies of the mid-1970s.

The third general finding that emerges from observing the legislative veto at work is that while the constitutional innovation had no appreciable impact on policy outcomes, and was invented to solve problems for which there already existed constitutional solutions, its presence had a mildly detrimental effect on members' fulfillment of their governing responsibilities. This is evident from looking at the consequences of its invalidation: the Supreme Court's restoration of separation of powers procedures led members to raise the visibility of their policy views, accept accountability for programs supported by broad consensus, and sharpen existing mechanisms for ensuring the openness to their constituents of the regulatory process.

By eliminating the legislative veto shortcut from Jackson-Vanik, the Supreme Court made it easier for members to raise the visibility of their objections to extending MFN to China after the Tiananmen Square massacre. Had the Supreme Court preserved the constitutionality of the legislative veto, members would not have been able to express their fury through the Jackson-Vanik disapproval resolution procedure. With legislative veto authority in place, using the disapproval resolution procedure would have led to outright termination of MFN for China, a policy for which there was little congressional support.

Similarly, once they lost formal access to the legislative veto shortcut in the Pell Grant statute, members turned their attention to accepting responsibility for their Pell Grant policy views. They lost patience with the pretense that the Department of Education would determine the needs analysis formula for distributing Pell Grant funds. Members had long exercised control over this formula because they held a strong bipartisan consensus regarding its proper scope. This consensus was simply hidden by the formal delegation to the department of policymaking authority in the Pell Grant statute. Members finally rescinded this authority, thereby bringing to light the congressional consensus about Pell Grant policy, when the Supreme Court's invalidation of the legislative veto disturbed the structure of delegation in the Pell Grant statute.

The invalidation of the legislative veto in GEPA shows how the Supreme Court's restoration of separation of powers led members to become more focused on opening up the regulatory process. They replaced the invalidated legislative veto with "negotiated rulemaking" provisions, thereby requiring the Department of Education to include members of regulated communities in rulemaking activities. Unlike the legislative veto, these provisions impose no legal restraints on the discretion of department officials to implement policies that members or their constituents find objectionable. The reg-neg procedure has nonetheless proven extremely popular among members, not surprisingly, because of its power to increase public access to the making of regulatory policy.

Had as much attention been focused on the legislative veto's practical insignificance as was accorded its questionable constitutionality, neither its opponents, like Chief Justice Burger, nor its advocates, like Justice White, would have believed that its invalidation would weaken congressional oversight power. But the legislative veto controversy was driven by what one member of Congress referred to as the mechanism's "sexiness."[2] As an amendment to constitutional procedure that promised to change policy outcomes by increasing congressional control over delegated authorities, the legislative veto possessed a unique capacity to attract widespread attention to matters of legislative and regulatory reform, matters that were "probably the least sexy subject in the world, so far as public interest is concerned."[3]

As a result, conventional wisdom about the workings of the legislative veto ignored the isolated voices of those who pointed out that the mechanism was actually inconsequential to determining policy outcomes. Former University of Chicago law professor Antonin Scalia, for example, warned that "however useful the veto may have been as a device to galvanize regulatory reform sentiment . . . our sentimental

CONCLUSION

attachment should not be permitted to distort our judgment that . . . the legislative veto is both ineffective in what it seeks to achieve and destructive of other values. . . . The legislative veto is a solution in search of a problem."[4] At the time, before the legislative veto was struck down as unconstitutional, Scalia's views received little attention among scholars and commentators. Members of Congress were the ones who occasionally gave public expression to his assertion that the mechanism was an ineffective oversight tool and that its popularity was due mostly to its symbolic power.[5]

Students of American politics would have been more likely to appreciate the real political significance of the legislative veto if they had had a better grasp of the principles embodied in the separation of powers system. Had they explored rather than denied the dynamic underlying American political institutions between liberty and popular sovereignty, on the one hand, and firm and effective governance on the other, legislative veto scholars would have seen that the mechanism's symbolic power as well as its practical irrelevance were, in fact, rather unsurprising.

Members were drawn to the constitutionally suspect legislative veto in the early 1970s because it provided them an easy way to give public expression to growing public distrust of the federal government's executive and regulatory powers. But members were reluctant to make actual use of an oversight mechanism that authorized Congress to evade the presidential veto. Members preferred to leave the responsibility for implementing public policy in the hands of executive branch officials. Without the responsibility for the actual administration of policy, members could remain free to voice their opinions on proposed policies, however extreme or unreasonable, wise or unpopular, their opinions might be. And in those situations where they were intent on exercising real control over delegated authorities, members were clearly not in need of any constitutional innovations.

The workings of the legislative veto, then, illuminate the practical consequences of the separation of powers system's dual objectives. At the same time that the system encourages public expression of varied and diverse political opinions, it discourages those opinions from resulting in substantive public policy changes unless those changes are likely to enjoy broad-based support when they are being implemented. In this way, the separation of powers both promotes representation and serves the demands of good governance.

By mischaracterizing the separation of powers as a system of "too tight ligaments," the Wilsonian framework made it easy to mistake the legislative veto's symbolic significance for actual policymaking power.[6] From the Wilsonian perspective, the mere fact of a shortcut through constitutional procedure was proof enough that the veto mechanism was playing an important role in determining public policy. And therein lies the key flaw of the dominant critique of American constitutionalism: rather than leaving open to question the viability of an eighteenth-century constitution in the twentieth century, the Wilsonian framework emphatically denies the possibility that the preservation of constitutional forms is consistent with institutional adaptation to changing political circumstances.[7]

In its impatience with constitutional forms, Wilson's political science reflected the spirit of his age. For a powerful strand of Progressivism, the dominant intellectual and political movement in the first quarter of the twentieth century, viewed the Constitution with contempt, as a "fossilized," obsolete "barrier to democratic national purpose."[8] In the late twentieth century, as newly emerging democracies are demanding new constitutions, and as the globalization of the economy produces new crises in governance, contemporary scholars of constitutional government are increasingly being led to ask, "Do Institutions Matter?" They are likely to find that the answer is: yes, but not in the rigid, deterministic way that the Progressive biases of the Wilsonian framework lead one to believe.[9]

Wilson was, of course, correct that the Framers of the Constitution could not have foreseen all of the governing responsibilities that the twentieth century would impose on American political institutions. But, in fact, the Framers themselves were well aware of their inability to foresee all the challenges that the future would bring, and, therefore, devised a system capable of responding to change. "Constitutions of civil government," they argued, "are not to be framed upon a calculation of existing exigencies, but upon a combination of these with the probable exigencies of ages, according to the natural and tried course of human affairs."[10]

Wilson surely overstated matters when he asserted of the Framers that "since they gave their work to the world the *whole face* of that world has changed."[11] Moreover, the fact of dramatic change does not, in and of itself, prove that the principles underlying constitutional structure have become irrelevant to contemporary politics. Neither does it prove that the separation of powers has served American citizens badly in the twentieth century. Those interested in evaluating whether the system fulfills contemporary governing needs should study American public policymaking through a framework that accurately describes the principles of constitutional structure. As is evident from re-examining the American separation of powers doctrine, such an account is readily available in the *Federalist Papers*. And, as is evident from re-examining the legislative veto controversy, the value of retrieving the Federalists' account is not to cheerlead for the Constitution but to make possible a better understanding of how it actually works.

Finally, the theory of American political institutions laid out in the *Federalist Papers* clarifies the place of the separation of powers itself within the overall system of American constitutional government. While the Framers had a keen appreciation for the political significance of institutional arrangements, they understood as well that institutions wer not the only matters of consequence for effective representative governance. The Framers' Constitution relies on American citizens to exercise sound judgment in choosing their representatives. Indeed, the proper exercise of the government's constitutional powers was itself predicated by the Framers on the "genius of the people of America."[12] But what is the character of this "genius"? How is it formed and preserved? Does the American political system foster the responsible choice it presupposes?

By design, American government depends upon both strong and flexible political institutions, and a free and responsible citizenry. Appreciation of this design can deepen our understanding of contemporary American politics, guiding us to the sources of governance failures, and also, perhaps, to unexpected strengths and advantages of constitutional democracy in America today.

NOTES

CHAPTER ONE. INTRODUCTION

1. See Stephen L. Elkin and Karol E. Soltan, eds., *A New Constitutionalism: Designing Political Institutions for a Good Society* (Chicago: University of Chicago Press, 1993); R. Kent Weaver and Bert A. Rockman, eds., *Do Institutions Matter? Government Capabilities in the United States and Abroad* (Washington, D.C.: The Brookings Institution, 1993).

2. In demanding centralization and expansion of federal power, Wilson's strand of Progressivism attacked the Constitution for its role in preserving the corrupt, decentralized, restraining character of the nineteenth-century party system. This attack also blamed the Constitution for the nation's inability to foster European-style bureaucracies; such bureaucracies would free administrative powers from political party control. See James W. Ceaser, *Presidential Selection: Theory and Development* (Princeton, N.J.: Princeton University Press, 1979), 170–212; Jeffrey Tulis, *The Rhetorical Presidency* (Princeton, N.J.: Princeton University Press, 1987), 118–37; John A. Rohr, *To Run a Constitution: The Legitimacy of the Administrative State* (Lawrence: University Press of Kansas, 1987), 55–75.

3. Wilson also believed that making Congress more like a parliament would weaken the existing party system and allow Congress to create powerful bureaucratic agencies. See Woodrow Wilson, *Congressional Government: A Study in American Politics* (1885; reprint ed., Gloucester, Mass.: Peter Smith, 1973); Woodrow Wilson, "Committee or Cabinet Government" (1884), in *Parliamentary versus Presidential Government*, ed. Arend Lijphart (New York: Oxford University Press, 1992).

4. Wilson's switch from, at first, advocating a unified, parliamentary-style legislature to, subsequently, advocating a "modern presidency" that would rely on rhetorical power to dominate Congress, produced two strands of intellectual descendants that are today directly opposed: one favors congressional prerogatives in policymaking, the other advocates unfettered executive power. See David K. Nichols, "Congressional Dominance and the Emergence of the Modern Presidency: Was Congress Ever the First Branch of Government?" in *Separation of Powers and Good Government*, ed. Bradford P. Wilson and Peter W. Schramm (Lanham, Md.: Rowman and Littlefield, 1994), 120–23, for extended analysis of this switch.

5. Austin Ranney, *Doctrine of Responsible Party Government* (Urbana: University of Illinois Press, 1954), 44. For in-depth analysis of the disjunction between Wilson's political science writings and his political career, see Daniel Stid, "Woodrow Wilson, Responsible Government, and the Founders' Regime" (Ph.D. diss., Harvard University, 1994).

6. For discussion of a wide range of proposed amendments to the separation of

powers system, see Donald L. Robinson, ed., *Reforming American Government: The Bicentennial Papers of the Committee on the Constitutional System* (Boulder, Colo.: Westview Press, 1985); Donald L. Robinson, *To the Best of My Ability: The Presidency and the Constitution* (New York: W. W. Norton, 1987), 259–82. Other legislative procedures enacted into law besides the legislative veto, like the provision granting the comptroller general the authority to determine the need for a sequestration of funds, have violated separation of powers procedures. See Chief Justice Burger's opinion in *Bowsher v Synar,* 478 US 714 (1986). But of such provisions that have actually been enacted into law, only the legislative veto provided scholars with five decades' worth of a track record to study.

7. For extended analysis of Hoover's experience with the legislative veto, see Joseph P. Harris, *Congressional Control of Administration* (Washington, D.C.: The Brookings Institution, 1964), 206–7; for discussion of the origins, development, and varied forms and uses of the veto mechanism, see, more generally, H. Lee Watson, *Congress Steps Out: A Look at Congressional Control of the Executive,* 63 California Law Review 983 (July 1975).

8. For analysis of the importance of the 1939 Reorganization Act, see Sidney M. Milkis, *The President and the Parties: The Transformation of the American Party System since the New Deal* (New York: Oxford University Press, 1993), 113–46.

9. For discussion of why, with respect to executive reorganization, the legislative veto never sustained the political significance it enjoyed in the 1939 Act, see Peri E. Arnold, *Making the Managerial Presidency: Comprehensive Reorganization Planning, 1905–1980* (Princeton, N.J.: Princeton University Press, 1986); Louis Fisher and Ronald C. Moe, "Presidential Reorganization Authority: Is It Worth the Cost?" *Political Science Quarterly* 96 (Summer 1981): 301–18. These studies include descriptions of how members of Congress learned, over time, that they did not need the veto mechanism to ensure control over reorganization authorities.

10. James L. Sundquist, *The Decline and Resurgence of Congress* (Washington, D.C.: The Brookings Institution, 1981), 354, describes the legislative veto as "the most forceful continuing expression of the congressional resurgence" of the 1970s.

11. For discussion of the "congressional resurgence" of the 1970s, see ibid.; Lawrence C. Dodd and Richard L. Schott, *Congress and the Administrative State* (New York: Wiley, 1979).

12. *Immigration and Naturalization Service (INS) v Chadha,* 462 US 919 (1983); Barbara Craig, *Chadha: The Story of an Epic Constitutional Struggle* (New York: Oxford University Press, 1988), 225, lists all the newspapers, including the *New York Times* and the *Washington Post,* that reported the Supreme Court's decision in *Chadha* on the front page.

13. See L. Gordon Crovitz and Jeremy A. Rabkin, eds., *The Fettered Presidency* (Washington, D.C.: American Enterprise Institute, 1989); Gordon S. Jones and John A. Marini, eds., *The Imperial Congress* (New York: Pharos Books, 1988).

14. Theodore B. Olson, "The Impetuous Vortex: Congressional Erosion of Presidential Authority," in Crovitz and Rabkin, *The Fettered Presidency,* 225–44.

15. Joseph Cooper, "The Legislative Veto in the 1980s," in *Congress Reconsidered*, ed. Lawrence C. Dodd and Bruce I. Oppenheimer, 3d ed. (Washington, D.C.: Congressional Quarterly, 1985), 364–89; James L. Sundquist, *Constitutional Reform and Effective Government* (Washington, D.C.: The Brookings Institution, 1986), 218–24.

16. Benjamin Ginsberg and Martin Shefter, *Politics by Other Means: The Declining Importance of Elections in America* (New York: Basic Books, 1990), 155, view the separation of powers jurisprudence articulated in *Chadha* as "portend[ing] the judiciary's emergence as a conservative bastion in alliance with the presidency."

17. With respect to the impact of *Chadha* on the Reagan administration's controversial foreign policies in particular, see "Congressional Checks Scuppered by Supreme Court," *Latin America Weekly Report*, 8 July 1983, 6; "Whose Business Is Central America?" *The Economist*, 9 July 1983, 19–20; Elizabeth Olson, "Court Scraps Legislative Veto," *United Press International*, 23 June 1983.

18. With such powers in the hands of bureaucrats rather than members of Congress, the American policymaking process becomes one of antidemocratic "interest group liberalism" rather than "juridical democracy." Theodore J. Lowi, *The End of Liberalism: Ideology, Policy, and the Crisis of Public Authority* (New York: Norton, 1969).

19. Cooper, "The Legislative Veto in the 1980s," 364.

20. *INS v Chadha*, 462 US 919, 972–73.

21. For review of functionalist legal scholarship, see Dean Alfange, Jr., *The Supreme Court and the Separation of Powers: A Welcome Return to Normalcy?* 58 George Washington Law Review 668 (April 1990).

22. Thomas M. Franck and Edward Weisband, *Foreign Policy by Congress* (New York: Oxford University Press, 1979), 76.

23. Wilson attacked the separation of powers because he believed it hindered the capacity of political institutions to insulate bureaucrats from political control. In this way, Woodrow Wilson was unlike some of his fellow Progressives, like Frank Goodnow, who argued that European-style bureaucracies could be created by insulating bureaucrats from political control through institutionalization of civil service reforms. Wilson always remained ambivalent about the value of creating bureaucracies within the American separation of powers system without first engaging in constitutional reform. See Stid, "Woodrow Wilson, Responsible Government, and the Founders' Regime." For historical analysis of debates over the capacity of the political system to institutionalize expertise, see Thomas McGraw, "Regulation in America: A Review Article," *Business History Review* 49 (Summer 1975): 159–83.

24. William N. Eskridge, Jr., and John Ferejohn, *The Article I, Section 7 Game*, 80 Georgetown Law Journal 523, 543 (February 1992).

25. For detailed analyses of the social and economic changes that forced Congress to create administrative agencies, see Lowi, *The End of Liberalism;* Stephen Skowronek, *Building a New American State: The Expansion of National Administrative Capacities, 1877–1920* (New York: Cambridge University Press, 1982).

26. For example, Sundquist, *Decline and Resurgence of Congress*, 35–36, argues that "when the U.S. Congress relinquishes authority to the executive, it

does not assign it to a committee of its own members under its ultimate control—as in a parliamentary country. . . . It tosses power over a barrier, so to speak, into alien territory."

27. David Schoenbrod, *Power without Responsibility: How Congress Abuses the People through Delegation* (New Haven, Conn.: Yale University Press, 1994), 94. Lowi, in *The End of Liberalism*, 301–2, argues that Woodrow Wilson's call for congressional delegation of authority was justified in a way that contemporary delegations are not because Wilson had in mind constitutional reforms that would make the American system more like a parliamentary government.

28. Schoenbrod, *Power without Responsibility*, 99.

29. Lowi, *The End of Liberalism*, 299.

30. Margaret Weir, Ann S. Orloff, and Theda Skocpol, eds., *The Politics of Social Policy in the United States* (Princeton, N.J.: Princeton University Press, 1988), 3.

31. Skowronek, *Building a New American State*, viii; see also Terry M. Moe, "The Politics of Bureaucratic Structure," in *Can the Government Govern?*, ed. John E. Chubb and Paul E. Peterson (Washington, D.C.: The Brookings Institution, 1989), 267–329.

32. See James L. Sundquist, ed., *Beyond Gridlock? Prospects for Governance in the Clinton Years—And After* (Washington, D.C.: The Brookings Institution, 1993).

33. For analysis of Nixon's admiration for Wilson, see Garry Wills, *Nixon Agonistes: The Crisis of the Self-Made Man* (Boston, Mass.: Houghton Mifflin, 1970), 419–95; for study of the ways in which Nixon attempted to bypass congressional policymaking powers, see Richard P. Nathan, *The Plot That Failed: Nixon and the Administrative Presidency* (New York: Wiley, 1975); see Forrest McDonald, *The American Presidency* (Lawrence: University Press of Kansas, 1994) for historical analysis of the ways in which students of American government have changed their minds about the virtues of strong executive power, depending on the political party of the particular president in question.

34. See Arthur M. Schlesinger, Jr., *The Imperial Presidency* (Boston, Mass.: Houghton Mifflin, 1973); Harold H. Koh, *The National Security Constitution: Sharing Power after the Iran-Contra Affair* (New Haven, Conn.: Yale University Press, 1990).

35. Those who hold this assumption also believe that delegations of congressional power are unconstitutional. See Schoenbrod, *Power without Responsibility*, 160–64; Bruce Ackerman, *We the People* (Cambridge, Mass.: Harvard University Press, 1991). But see Donald R. Brand, *Corporatism and the Rule of Law: A Study of the National Recovery Administration* (Ithaca, N.Y.: Cornell University Press, 1988) and Sotirios A. Barber, *The Constitution and the Delegation of Congressional Power* (Chicago: University of Chicago Press, 1975) who show that Chief Justice Marshall, President Washington, and Washington's cabinet, all believed congressional delegation was perfectly constitutional and necessary.

36. For an overview of the consequences for contemporary political analysis of Wilson's understanding of presidential power, see James W. Ceaser, "Doctrines of Presidential-Congressional Relations," in Wilson and Schramm, *Separation of Powers and Good Government*, 110.

37. James Q. Wilson, *Bureaucracy: What Government Agencies Do and Why They Do It* (New York: Basic Books, 1989), 235–53, analyzes the statutory control mechanisms—all perfectly constitutional—that members of Congress have developed to restrain bureaucrats from exercising unchecked powers; for discussion of "action-forcing statutes" see Martin Shapiro, *Who Guards the Guardians? Judicial Control of Administration* (Athens: University of Georgia Press, 1988), 80–87; R. Shep Melnick, *Regulation and the Courts: The Case of the Clean Air Act* (Washington, D.C.: The Brookings Institution, 1983); Robert A. Katzmann, *Institutional Disability: The Saga of Transportation Policy for the Disabled* (Washington, D.C.: The Brookings Institution, 1986).

38. For analysis of the sources of this judicial activism, see Shapiro, *Who Guards the Guardians?;* Richard B. Stewart, *The Reformation of American Administrative Law,* 88 Harvard Law Review 1667 (June 1975).

39. For a discussion of the causes and development of this decentralization, see Joel D. Aberbach, *Keeping a Watchful Eye: The Politics of Congressional Oversight* (Washington, D.C.: The Brookings Institution, 1990), 19–75; for more specific examples and personal accounts of structural changes within Congress since the 1960s that have profoundly increased congressional power vis-à-vis the executive branch, see Joseph A. Califano, Jr., "The Imperial Congress," *The New York Times Magazine,* 23 January 1994, 40. None of these changes analyzed by Aberbach or Califano required constitutional reform.

40. Arend Lijphart, *Democracies* (New Haven, Conn.: Yale University Press, 1984), 78.

41. For further explanation, see R. Kent Weaver and Bert A. Rockman, "Assessing the Effects of Institutions," in *Do Institutions Matter?,* 14–15.

42. Barbara Hinckley, *Less Than Meets the Eye: Foreign Policymaking and the Myth of the Assertive Congress* (Chicago: University of Chicago Press, 1994); Robert A. Katzmann, "War Powers: Toward a New Accommodation," in *A Question of Balance,* ed. Thomas E. Mann (Washington, D.C.: The Brookings Institution, 1990), 135–69; Paul E. Peterson, "The President's Dominance in Foreign Policymaking," *Political Science Quarterly* 109 (Summer 1994): 215–34.

43. In *Less Than Meets the Eye,* Hinckley shows that this unfounded view (that members of Congress would have much more direct and immediate control over the administration of foreign policy if they only had greater constitutional powers), is widely accepted in contemporary scholarly and journalistic analyses of Congress and foreign policymaking. Gordon Silverstein in *Imbalance of Powers: Constitutional Interpretation and the Making of American Foreign Policy* (New York: Oxford University Press, forthcoming, 1996) shows that members of Congress have not taken advantage of their constitutional powers to react against the aggregation of foreign policymaking power in the presidency. They have, instead, preferred to defer to the president.

CHAPTER TWO. THE AMERICAN SEPARATION OF POWERS DOCTRINE

1. This includes not only domestic constitutional reformers and critics of American public policy but also students of comparative politics; see Sven H. Steinmo,

"American Exceptionalism Reconsidered: Culture or Institutions?" in *The Dynamics of American Politics: Approaches and Interpretations,* ed. Lawrence C. Dodd and Calvin Jillson (Boulder, Colo.: Westview Press, 1994), 106–31; Philip G. Cerny, "Political Entropy and American Decline," *Millennium: Journal of International Studies* 18 (Spring 1988): 47–63; and Martin Harrop, ed., *Power and Policy in Liberal Democracies* (Cambridge: Cambridge University Press, 1992).

2. Samuel P. Huntington, *Political Order in Changing Societies* (New Haven, Conn.: Yale University Press, 1968), 110–11; Huntington traces this view to the writings of Walter Bagehot, the nineteenth-century British constitutional theorist whom Woodrow Wilson considered "our most astute English critic." Woodrow Wilson, *Congressional Government: A Study in American Politics* (1885; reprint ed., Gloucester, Mass.: Peter Smith, 1973), 202.

3. Woodrow Wilson, *Constitutional Government in the United States* (1908; New York: Columbia University Press, 1961), 54–55; to trace the importance of this view in twentieth-century political science, see John A. Rohr, *To Run a Constitution: The Legitimacy of the Administrative State* (Lawrence: University Press of Kansas, 1986); and Raymond Seidelman, *Disenchanted Realists: Political Science and the American Crisis, 1884–1984* (Albany: State University of New York Press, 1985); James W. Ceaser, *Liberal Democracy and Political Science* (Baltimore, Md.: Johns Hopkins University Press, 1990) traces the origins of this Wilsonian presumption back to the political struggles of the Jeffersonian Republicans and the anti-Jacksonian Whigs. Wilson's innovation was in denouncing rather than applauding the separation of powers system's supposed inability to enable efficient governance.

4. Charles C. Thach, Jr., *The Creation of the Presidency, 1775–1789: A Study in Constitutional History* (1923; reprint ed., New York: Da Capo Press, 1969), 57.

5. Ibid., 62.

6. Louis Fisher, "The Efficiency Side of Separated Powers," *Journal of American Studies* 5 (August 1971): 115.

7. George Washington, *The Writings of George Washington,* ed. John C. Fitzpatrick, vol. 30 (Washington, D.C.: Government Printing Office, 1939), 300–301; cited in Fisher, "Efficiency Side of Separated Powers," 117.

8. Brutus, cited in Herbert J. Storing, with the assistance of Murray Dry, *What the Anti-Federalists Were For* (Chicago: University of Chicago Press, 1981), 60.

9. See Aristotle's analysis of "regimes" in *The Politics,* book 4, trans. Carnes Lord (Chicago: University of Chicago Press, 1984). For analysis of Aristotelian constitutionalism and its influence on the American Framers, see Harvey C. Mansfield, Jr.'s "Separation of Powers in the American Constitution," in *America's Constitutional Soul* (Baltimore, Md.: Johns Hopkins University Press, 1991), 115–27, and *Taming the Prince: The Ambivalence of Modern Executive Power* (New York: The Free Press, 1989); see also W. B. Gwyn, *The Meaning of the Separation of Powers: An Analysis of the Doctrine from Its Origin to the Adoption of the United States Constitution* (New Orleans, La.: Tulane University Press, 1965) and Samuel H. Beer, *To Make a Nation: The Rediscovery of American Federalism* (Cambridge, Mass.: Harvard University Press, 1993).

10. These *Federalist Papers* were written by Alexander Hamilton, James Madison, and John Jay, writing under the pseudonym Publius, to rally support for the new Constitution.

11. Alexander Hamilton, James Madison, and John Jay, *The Federalist Papers*, ed. Clinton Rossiter (New York: Mentor, 1961), #70, 424. The bicameralism and presentment clauses, requiring that any bill be passed by two chambers of Congress and be subject to an overridable presidential veto, are two means by which Publius meant to ensure that laws enacted by Congress would reflect the "deliberation and wisdom" rather than the "passions" of the people. See #62, justifying the creation of a Senate and #73, justifying the presidential veto.

12. Ibid., #70, 424, 423.

13. Ibid., #78, 471.

14. Ibid., #78, 471–72.

15. Ibid., #48, 308.

16. Ibid., #37, 228; for in-depth analysis of the seeming contradiction between Publius's discussion of the "nature" of different types of powers, and his claim that it is not possible to distinguish them "with sufficient certainty," see William Kristol, "The Problem of the Separation of Powers: *Federalist 47–51*," in *Saving the Revolution: The Federalist Papers and the American Founding*, ed. Charles R. Kesler (New York: The Free Press, 1987), 100–130.

17. Gwyn, *The Meaning of the Separation of Powers*, 108.

18. Charles-Louis de Secondat, Baron de Montesquieu, *The Spirit of the Laws*, trans. and ed. Anne M. Cohler, Basia Carolyn Miller, and Harold Samuel Stone (Avon, U.K.: Cambridge University Press, 1989), 157.

19. "The Address and Reasons of Dissent of the Minority of the Convention of Pennsylvania to Their Constituents," in *The Complete Anti-Federalist*, ed. Herbert J. Storing, with the assistance of Murray Dry (Chicago: University of Chicago Press, 1981), 3:161.

20. Ibid.

21. *The Federalist Papers*, #47, 301. James Madison called the separation of powers a "first principle of free government." Cited in Gordon S. Wood, *The Creation of the American Republic, 1776–1787* (New York: Norton, 1969), 152.

22. *The Federalist Papers*, #47, 301.

23. Ibid., #47, 304; #51, 321–22.

24. Ibid., #48, 308.

25. Wilson, *Congressional Government*, 28.

26. Ibid., 54.

27. Ibid., 31.

28. Ibid., 203.

29. Ibid., 206.

30. David F. Epstein, *The Political Theory of The Federalist* (Chicago: University of Chicago Press, 1984), 146.

31. *The Federalist Papers*, #51, 322.

32. Ibid., #39, 240, 241.

33. Ibid., #1, 35; #76, 455.

34. Ibid., #37, 226; for further discussion, see Jeffrey Leigh Sedgwick,

"James Madison and the Problem of Executive Character," *Polity* 21 (Fall 1988): 5–23.

35. Ibid., #62, 379; #10, 77.

36. Ibid., #63, 385; #10, 77.

37. Ibid., #70, 423; #62, 379; #78, 470; #1, 35.

38. Ibid., #49, 313.

39. Ibid., #49, 315; #62, 381; #49, 314, 315.

40. Ibid., #63, 384.

41. Publius's insight about the interdependence of effective governance and popular sovereignty finds dramatic resonance in twentieth-century war history. John Kenneth Galbraith notes, for example, that Nazi Germany proved less capable of imposing the sacrifices necessary for mobilizing a war economy than Britain, France, or the United States. With "democratic communication . . . government knew what the people could and would take. . . . In Germany there was no similar communication between people and state; the government, in consequence, was more circumspect in imposing sacrifice. This was one of the previously unperceived disadvantages of dictatorship." *A Journey through Economic Time: A Firsthand View* (Boston: Houghton Mifflin, 1994), 127–28. For discussion, more generally, of why democracies are better than dictatorships at forging public policies that promote economic growth, see "Democracy and Growth: Why Voting Is Good for You," *The Economist*, 27 August 1994, 15–17.

42. *Myers v United States*, 272 US 52, 293 (1926). Though Brandeis's dictum has often been used to justify the view that constitutional forms were intended to hinder good governance, Brandeis himself did not believe that the separation of powers system was solely intended to impose automatic, "Newtonian" checks on the exercise of governmental powers. He expected the constitutional system to "fit its rulers for their task," demanding from them, "in the main, education and character," so that they would best fulfill the various responsibilities of governing. Excerpted in *The Brandeis Guide to the Modern World*, ed. Alfred Lief (Boston: Little, Brown & Company, 1941), 4.

43. Chapter 3 elaborates on this point.

44. Donald Robinson, cofounder of CCS, quoted in *Beyond Gridlock: Prospects for Governance in the Clinton Years—and After*, ed. James L. Sundquist (Washington, D.C.: The Brookings Institution, 1993), 57.

45. Cutler, "To Form a Government," in *Reforming American Government*, ed. Donald L. Robinson (Boulder, Colo.: Westview Press, 1985), 12, 13.

46. Robert A. Dahl, *A Preface to Democratic Theory* (Chicago: University of Chicago Press, 1956), 22.

47. Ibid., 31.

48. In his recent essay on the infirmities of American politics, Dahl has explicitly stepped away from the Wilsonian framework supported by his earlier work. He notes now that "we lack the theory and evidence that might justify the conclusion that the people of the United States would be markedly better off if, say, they were to replace presidential government and the two-party system with a parliamentary government, PR [proportional representation], and a multiparty system. For all we know, the American people might indeed be better off. Or worse. Or about the same." Robert A. Dahl, *The New American Political (Dis)Order* (Berkeley, Calif.: Institute of Governmental Studies Press, 1994), 20.

49. For a practical example of the kind of policy failure that Publius attempted to avoid by separating powers, see David Butler, Andrew Adonis, and Tony Travers, *Failure in British Government: The Politics of the Poll Tax* (New York: Oxford University Press, 1994), which describes how the fused executive and legislative powers in the British Cabinet enabled the government to enact a profound policy change, the poll tax, in spite of widespread objections from local government treasurers who realized and predicted that it would be a disaster, which it soon proved to be. See also, "Britain's Constitution: The Case for Reform," *The Economist,* 14 October 1985, 25, which argues that "Britain's government is overcentralised and insufficiently accountable."

50. For further discussion of SALT II in this regard, see James Q. Wilson, "Does the Separation of Powers Still Work?" *The Public Interest* (Winter 1987): 36–52. For Publius's explanation of how it is in the best interest of the nation to split the treaty-making power between the president and the Senate, see *The Federalist Papers,* #64, #75.

51. Sven Steinmo and Jon Watts, "It's the Institutions, Stupid! Why Comprehensive National Health Insurance Always Fails in America," *Journal of Health Politics, Policy and Law* 20 (Summer 1995): 329–72; but, in response, see William Schneider, "Health Care: So Where's the Crisis?," *National Journal* 26 (11 June 1994): 1378, who compares the failure of the Clinton plan to the success of other comprehensive reform proposals in American history; and, especially, Theda Skocpol, "The Rise and Resounding Demise of the Clinton Plan," *Health Affairs* 14 (Spring 1995): 81, who explains, with detailed historical analysis, that "if progressives are actually to achieve universal health care coverage in America, it will be because new rationales for the role of government, and new majority political alliances, have been achieved first. I believe that such new rationales and alliances can be forged."

52. Martin Diamond, "Conservatives, Liberals, and the Constitution," in *As Far as Republican Principles Will Admit,* ed. William A. Schambra (Washington, D.C.: American Enterprise Institute, 1992), 85, notes that "the liberal complaint that majorities cannot act has no foundation; the real complaint is that majorities simply do not act as liberal conviction requires." For empirical support of this observation, see Morris Fiorina, *Divided Government* (New York: Macmillan, 1992), 88; and Hans-Dieter Klingemann, Richard I. Hofferbert, and Ian Budge, *Parties, Policies, and Democracy* (Boulder, Colo.: Westview Press, 1994), 138, who find that in comparison to political parties in ten different countries, American political parties are "equally able to bring into effect their programs in government, despite institutional fragmentation—owing above all to the central position and pivotal forces of the presidency within the federal system."

53. James W. Ceaser argues, in *Liberal Democracy and Political Science,* 195, that "critics of separation of powers often mistakenly equate governing with policymaking. . . . Commentators may fill all the pages they please about health policy, industrial policy, or urban policy, but these concerns in no way diminish either the need to use political power with energy and discretion at critical moments or the necessity of watching and checking that same power."

54. Daniel Stid, "Woodrow Wilson, Responsible Government, and the Founders' Regime" (Ph.D. diss., Harvard University, 1994), 309.

55. Diary of Dr. Grayson, 11 December 1918, *The Papers of Woodrow Wilson*, ed. Arthur S. Link, 69 vols. (Princeton, N.J.: Princeton University Press, 1966–1994), 53:365; cited in Stid, "Woodrow Wilson," 310.

56. For sympathetic presentation of this perspective and review of those who hold it, see Terry Eastland, *Energy in the Executive: The Case for the Strong Presidency* (New York: The Free Press, 1992). For a critique of this view that blames the Wilsonian framework as the source of its shortcomings, see David K. Nichols, *The Myth of the Modern Presidency* (University Park: Pennsylvania State University Press, 1994). See also, Arthur M. Schlesinger, Jr., *The Cycles of American History* (Boston: Houghton Mifflin, 1986), 280, who describes how an "Imperial Presidency" demands the elimination of "Congress as a serious partner in the constitutional order," by quoting Nixon's memoirs: Nixon recalled that "my reading of history taught me that when all the leadership institutions of a nation become paralyzed by self-doubt and second thoughts, that nation cannot long survive unless those institutions are either reformed, replaced, or circumvented. In my second term I was prepared to adopt whichever of these three methods—or whichever combination of them—was necessary."

57. In his classic analysis of the Vietnam disaster, *On Strategy: A Critical Analysis of the Vietnam War* (Novato, Calif.: Presidio Press, 1982), Harry G. Summers, Jr., argues that national defense strategies that lack the formal, broad-based support that comes with congressional legislation, will, in the long run, fail to achieve their objectives no matter how extensive or unlimited the presidential powers available to try to implement them.

58. For examples of such cases, see Robert S. Gilmour and Alexis A. Halley, eds., *Who Makes Public Policy? The Struggle for Control between Congress and the Executive* (Chatham, N.J.: Chatham House Publishers, 1994).

59. Theodore J. Lowi, *The End of Liberalism: Ideology, Policy, and the Crisis of Public Authority* (New York: Norton, 1969), 156.

60. Thomas Schwartz, "Publius and Public Choice," in *The Federalist Papers and the New Institutionalism*, ed. Bernard Grofman and Donald Wittman (New York: Agathon Press, 1989), 35.

61. See William N. Eskridge, Jr., and John Ferejohn, *The Article I, Section 7 Game*, 80 Georgetown Law Journal 523 (February 1992); also Jack Knight, *Positive Models and Normative Theory: A Comment on Eskridge and Ferejohn*, 8 Journal of Law, Economics, & Organization 190, 193 (March 1992); and Daniel B. Rodriguez, *The Administrative State and the Original Understanding: Comments on Eskridge and Ferejohn*, ibid., 197, 198 (March 1992).

62. For a critique of Lowi's presumption that broad delegations of congressional power are undemocratic and antithetical to representative government in the United States, see Harvey C. Mansfield, Jr., "Disguised Liberalism," in *The Spirit of Liberalism* (Cambridge, Mass.: Harvard University Press, 1978), 28–51; and Jerry L. Mashaw, *Prodelegation: Why Administrators Should Make Political Decisions,* 1 Journal of Law, Economics, & Organization 81 (Spring 1985).

63. See Anne M. Khademian, *The SEC and Capital Market Regulation: The Politics of Expertise* (Pittsburgh, Pa.: University of Pittsburgh Press, 1992); for

in-depth discussion of the meaning of "effectiveness," see Patrick Wolf, "What History Advises about Reinventing Government: A Meta-Analysis of Bureaucratic Effectiveness in U.S. Federal Agencies" (Ph.D. diss., Harvard University, 1995), 1–15; see also Donald R. Brand, *Corporatism and the Rule of Law: A Study of the National Recovery Administration* (Ithaca, N.Y.: Cornell University Press, 1988), whose analysis of the policies of the National Recovery Administration—policies that were struck down by the Supreme Court as violating the "nondelegation doctrine"—shows that the problems described by Lowi's critique were not, in fact, due to congressional delegation. Brand provides evidence, furthermore, that forcing Congress to refrain from delegating authority would "hamper rather than facilitate effective governance" (312). For theoretical support to Brand's claim that the problems critics attribute to congressional delegation would not, in fact, be solved by preventing Congress from delegating authority, see Mancur Olson's *The Logic of Collective Action: Public Goods and the Theory of Groups* (Cambridge, Mass.: Harvard University Press, 1965) and *The Rise and Decline of Nations: Economic Growth, Stagflation, and Social Rigidities* (New Haven, Conn.: Yale University Press, 1982), which suggest that the infirmities of "interest-group liberalism" attacked by Lowi's critique are better explained by examining the character of policymaking in stable democracies than by the particular institutional locus of policymaking power.

64. It remains to be seen how successful the recently elected Republican majority in Congress will be in enacting its explicit commitments to eliminate, cut, and restructure agencies, regulations, and entitlements that it deems ineffective. If nothing else, however, these commitments are a striking reminder of Congress's authority to completely rearrange public policy if it so chooses. It is worth noting, furthermore, that already by the late 1980s, the power of well-heeled interest groups to protect the particularistic benefits they were deriving from public policy had declined measurably. This decline of "interest-group liberalism" is the subject of Gary Mucciaroni's *Reversals of Fortune: Public Policy and Private Interests* (Washington, D.C.: The Brookings Institution, 1995).

65. "A Presidential Address to the American Political Science Association," 27 December 1910, *The Papers of Woodrow Wilson*, 22:271.

66. Editorial note on *Congressional Government*, ibid., 4:6.

67. "At no time during the research for and writing of *Congressional Government* did Wilson go to Washington to observe Congress at first hand" (ibid., 12); for an example of Wilson's dismissal of the need to engage in any actual research, see Woodrow Wilson to Ellen Louise Axson, 22 January 1885, ibid., 3:630.

68. Woodrow Wilson to Richard Heath Dabney, 28 October 1885, ibid., 5:37–38.

CHAPTER THREE. THE LEGISLATIVE VETO

1. This was recounted to the author by Professor Koh in New Haven, Conn., September 1990.

2. *Immigration and Naturalization Service (INS) v Chadha*, 462 US 919

(1983). Decided 7–2 with Chief Justice Burger writing the majority opinion and Justice White writing the dissent.

3. This view is based on an exaggerated reading, as will be discussed below, of the findings of Louis Fisher, *The Legislative Veto: Invalidated, It Survives,* 56 Law and Contemporary Problems 273 (Autumn 1993).

4. James L. Sundquist, *The Decline and Resurgence of Congress* (Washington, D.C.: The Brookings Institution, 1981), 354.

5. Advocates of the legislative veto's constitutionality argued that the mechanism did not constitute full-scale legislative action. The majority in *Chadha* asserted that it did. For analysis of the way in which the majority overcame this complication, see Peter L. Strauss, *Was There a Baby in the Bathwater? A Comment on the Supreme Court's Legislative Veto Decision,* 1983 Duke Law Journal 789 (September 1983).

6. The bicameralism requirement, U.S. Constitution, Article I, §1, vests "all legislative Powers . . . in a Congress of the United States, which shall consist of a Senate and House of Representatives." The presentment clause, Art. I, §7, states that "every Bill which shall have passed the House of Representatives and the Senate shall, before it become a Law, be presented to the President of the United States."

7. *INS v Chadha,* 462 US 919, 978.

8. Ibid., 968.

9. Ibid., 972.

10. Dean Alfange, Jr., *The Supreme Court and the Separation of Powers: A Welcome Return to Normalcy?* 58 George Washington Law Review 668, 670 (April 1990).

11. Ibid., 671.

12. Stephen Breyer, *The Legislative Veto after Chadha,* 72 Georgetown Law Journal 785, 790 (February 1984).

13. One strand of critiques blames the separation of powers for allowing Congress to make open-ended delegations to executive branch and independent agencies, thereby violating democratic principles by leaving unchecked powers in the hands of unelected bureaucrats. Another strand criticizes the tripartite system for hindering the capacity for policy leadership in American government. To remedy the problem, it recommends either subsuming administrative responsibilities under legislative control by amending the American system into a British-style parliamentary system, or further freeing administration from legislative control by subjecting Congress to executive branch dominance. This is elaborated in chapter 2.

14. Joseph Cooper, "The Legislative Veto in the 1980s," in *Congress Reconsidered,* ed. Lawrence C. Dodd and Bruce I. Oppenheimer, 3d ed. (Washington, D.C.: Congressional Quarterly Press, 1985), 364.

15. *INS v Chadha,* 462 US 919, 967–68, 972.

16. Ibid., 945.

17. Ibid., 944.

18. Of all the voluminous writings on the constitutionality and desirability of the legislative veto mechanism, Justice Scalia's comments—articulated at a time,

in the mid-1970s, when the legislative veto was becoming increasingly notewor-thy as an issue that promised to have serious consequences for American public policy—remain the wisest and most prescient. At the same time that he articu-lated clear constitutional objections to the legislative veto, he also explained that he did not expect it to be of much consequence in the policymaking process because he understood Congress's extensive oversight powers to be perfectly con-stitutional. Many of those who shared his objections, however, failed to preserve the subtlety of his analysis in their denunciation of the legislative veto and ebul-lient support for *Chadha*. For an example of Scalia's perspective on the legisla-tive veto, see Antonin Scalia, "The Legislative Veto: A False Remedy for System Overload," *American Enterprise Institute Journal on Government and Society* (November–December 1979):19–26.

19. Charles J. Cooper, *How Separation of Powers Protects Individual Liber-ties,* in L. Gordon Crovitz, Moderator, 41 Rutgers Law Review 785, 792 (Spring 1989).

20. Stuart M. Statler, Consumer Product Safety Commission, in Administrative Conference of the United States, *Legislative Veto of Agency Rules after INS v Chadha,* Twenty-Seventh Plenary Session Discussion, 15 December 1983, Ap-pendix A, 12.

21. C. Boyden Gray, "Special Interests, Regulation, and the Separation of Powers," in *The Fettered Presidency: Legal Constraints on the Executive Branch,* ed. L Gordon Crovitz and Jeremy A. Rabkin (Washington, D.C.: American En-terprise Institute, 1989), 221.

22. House Committee on Public Works and Transportation, *Amendments to the Metropolitan Washington Airports Authority Act of 1986: Hearing before the Sub-committee on Aviation of the Committee on Public Works and Transportation,* 102d Cong., 1st sess., 26 September 1991, 148 (Johnny H. Killian, Congressio-nal Research Service).

23. *Congressional Record,* 100th Cong., 2d sess., 134, no. 50, daily ed. (19 April 1988): 1713 (Rep. Robert Walker, R-PA).

24. House Committee on Rules, *Regulatory Reform and Congressional Review of Agency Rules: Hearings before the Subcommittee on Rules of the House of the Committee on Rules,* 96th Cong., 1st sess., pt. 1, 11 July 1979, 10.

25. In researching this chapter, the author conducted several interviews, in the period between September 1990 and May 1992, with current and former officials of the Justice Department, Office of Management and Budget, Environmental Protection Agency, and White House Counsel, congressional staff from House and Senate legal counsel's offices and appropriations committees, and lobbyists representing farming industries and public-interest law groups. The names of the interviewees are not mentioned in order to maintain confidentiality.

26. In his opinion, 37 Op. Att'y Gen. 56, 63–64 (1933), Mitchell noted that the legislative veto provision enacted into the previous year's Reorganization Act was also unconstitutional, raising "a grave question as to the validity of the entire provision . . . for Executive reorganization of governmental functions." Hoover himself had not quite understood the legislative veto procedure that Congress succeeded in getting him to sign into law in 1932. Hoover became hostile to the

procedure within a year after signing the 1932 provision into law, took Mitchell's advice to heart, and never again signed a veto provision into law. See Herbert Hoover, *The Memoirs of Herbert Hoover: The Cabinet and the Presidency, 1920–1933,* vol. 2 (New York: Macmillan, 1952), 283–84, cited in Thomas Franck and Clifford Bob, *The Return of Humpty-Dumpty: Foreign Relations Law after the Chadha Case,* 79 American Journal of International Law, 912, 918 (October 1985).

27. See, for example, President Franklin Roosevelt's confidential objection to the veto provision, published posthumously in Robert H. Jackson, *A Presidential Legal Opinion,* 66 Harvard Law Review 1353 (June 1953); for a listing of presidential objections, see House Committee on the Judiciary, *Congressional Review of Administrative Rulemaking: Hearings before the Subcommittee on Administrative Law and Governmental Relations of the Committee on the Judiciary,* 94th Cong., 1st sess., 29 October 1975, 379 (Antonin Scalia, Assistant Attorney General).

28. Barbara Hinkson Craig, *Chadha: The Story of an Epic Constitutional Struggle* (New York: Oxford University Press, 1988), 53.

29. James L. Sundquist, *Constitutional Reform and Effective Government* (Washington, D.C.: The Brookings Institution, 1986), 218.

30. *Chadha v Immigration and Naturalization Service (INS),* 634 F2d 408 (9th Cir. 1980).

31. Craig, *Chadha,* 88; for discussion of legislative veto cases that the Department of Justice chose not to pursue as test cases for challenging the veto in the Supreme Court, see ibid., 90–93.

32. *Chadha v. INS,* 634 F2d 408, 411.

33. The resolution opposing permanent residence for six aliens, including Mr. Chadha, was passed by voice vote on the floor of the House, before it was even printed or made available to members. It was introduced by Rep. Joshua Eilberg (D-PA), Chairman of the Judiciary Subcommittee on Immigration, Citizenship, and International Law, who claimed that the six aliens in question had not met the requirement of "hardship" and that "their deportation should not be suspended." *Congressional Record,* 94th Cong., 1st sess., 1975, 121, pt. 31:40800; see also Craig, *Chadha,* 3–35.

34. H.Res. 926, in *Congressional Record,* 94th Cong., 1st sess., 1975, 121, pt. 31:40800.

35. *Chadha v INS,* 634 F2d 408.

36. Quoted in Craig, *Chadha,* 25.

37. See above, note 25.

38. Craig, *Chadha,* 101, notes that the Justice Department and public-interest lawyers who were together working to have the legislative veto invalidated were ambivalent about taking the Ninth Circuit *Chadha* case to the Supreme Court because "a win in *Chadha* might not help accomplish their real aim—to get rid of legislative vetoes over regulations." For analysis of the regulatory legislative veto provision from the Natural Gas Policy Act pending in court at the time, see ibid., 115–47.

39. See above, note 25.

40. While the provision at issue in the INA statute, a one-house veto, authorized a single chamber to veto executive branch actions, the majority's reasoning in *Chadha* allowed the Supreme Court to declare two-house vetoes unconstitutional in subsequent cases without giving any further explanations. Two-house vetoes complied with the bicameralism clause, but they were unconstitutional according to *Chadha* because they bypassed the presentment requirement. See *Process Gas Consumers Group v Consumer Energy Council of America*, 463 US 1216 (1983), affirming *Consumer Energy Council of America v Federal Energy Regulatory Commission (FERC)*, 673 F2d 425 (D.C. Cir. 1982); and *United States Senate v Federal Trade Commission (FTC)*, 463 US 1216 (1983), affirming *Consumers Union of U.S. Inc. v Federal Trade Commission (FTC)*, 691 F2d 575 (D.C. Cir. 1982). All committee vetoes (where an individual congressional committee, or a set of committees, were vested with the authority to prohibit particular agency actions, or to waive required waiting periods) were thus deemed unconstitutional because committee vetoes violate both bicameralism and presentment. Joint resolutions remained constitutional, however, because approving or disapproving agency activities by means of joint resolutions requires both chambers to pass the resolution which must itself be presented to the president.

41. *INS v Chadha*, 462 US 919, 959.

42. Ibid., 1002.

43. House Committee on Rules, *Legislative Veto after Chadha: Hearings before the Committee on Rules*, 98th Cong., 2d sess., 9 November 1983, 28 (Senator Carl Levin, D-MI).

44. Elliott H. Levitas and Stanley M. Brand, *The Post Legislative Veto Response: A Call to Congressional Arms*, 12 Hofstra Law Review 593, 616 (Spring 1984).

45. Paul C. Light, "The Focusing Skill and Presidential Influence in Congress," in *Congressional Politics*, ed. Christopher Deering (Pacific Grove, Calif.: Brooks/Cole Publishing, 1989), 254.

46. See Arthur S. Miller and George Knapp, *The Congressional Veto: Preserving the Constitutional Framework*, 52 Indiana Law Journal 367, 371 (Spring 1977); and lists of legislative veto provisions prepared by the CRS, reprinted in House Committee on Rules, *Congressional Review of Agency Rulemaking: Hearings before the Subcommittee on Rules of the House of the Committee on Rules*, 97th Cong., 1st sess., 7, 28 October and 19 November 1981, 321–57; see, also, summary of legislative veto lists prepared in the 1970s by the CRS and by political scientists, in Barbara Hinkson Craig, *The Legislative Veto: Congressional Control of Regulation* (Boulder, Colo.: Westview Press, 1983), 1–43.

47. *INS v Chadha*, 462 US 919, 955.

48. Girardeau A. Spann, *Spinning the Legislative Veto*, 72 Georgetown Law Journal 813, 815 (February 1984); Breyer, *Legislative Veto after Chadha*, 792.

49. E. Donald Elliott, "INS v. Chadha: The Administrative Constitution, The Constitution and the Legislative Veto," in *The Supreme Court Review: 1983* (Chicago: University of Chicago Press, 1984), 147.

50. Spann, *Spinning the Legislative Veto*, 815.

51. Joseph Cooper, "Postscript on the Congressional Veto: Is There Life After *Chadha?*" *Political Science Quarterly* 98 (Fall 1983): 427–29; Michael Horan,

Adjusting the Separation of Powers: The "Legislative Veto" and the United States Supreme Court's Decision in the Chadha Case, 14 Anglo American Law Review 205 (April–May 1985); Robert F. Nagel, *The Legislative Veto, the Constitution, and the Courts,* 3 Constitutional Commentary 61 (Winter 1986).

52. House Committee on Rules, *Legislative Veto after Chadha,* 9 November 1983, 17.

53. Ibid., 20.

54. *INS v Chadha,* 462 US 919, 935 n. 9.

55. Morton Rosenberg and Jack H. Maskell, *Congressional Intervention in the Administrative Process: Legal and Ethical Considerations,* CRS Report for Congress 90-440 (Washington, D.C.: Congressional Research Service, 1990), 31; Raymond J. Celada, "Constitutionality of Providing a Statutory Basis for General Accounting Office Bid Protest System," CRS Report to Senate Committee on Governmental Affairs, Subcommittee on Oversight and Management, in *Congressional Record,* 99th Cong., 1st sess., 131, no. 127, daily ed. (3 October 1985): 12525–27. The D.C. Circuit Court recently affirmed that report-and-wait provisions are constitutional because they allow the agency in question to proceed with its proposed policies in spite of the informal objections of a congressional committee chair, or other such legislative agent. *Hechinger v Metropolitan Washington Airports Authority* 36 F3d 97, 103–4 (D.C. Cir. 1994), cert. denied 23 January 1995.

56. Rosenberg and Maskell, *Congressional Intervention,* 30; Brett G. Kappel, *Judicial Restrictions on Improper Congressional Influence in Administrative Decision-making: A Defense of the Pillsbury Doctrine,* 6 Journal of Law and Politics 135, 137 (Fall 1989).

57. *City of Alexandria v United States,* 3 Cl.Ct. 667, 683 (1983).

58. *City of Alexandria v United States,* 737 F2d 1022, 1025 (Fed. Cir. 1984).

59. Ibid.

60. This presumption, that informal interbranch dealings violate the separation of powers, is responsible for contemporary claims that Congress has failed to comply with *Chadha.* See below for critique of this misguided claim. Some of the recent public choice scholarship on congressional oversight explicitly avoids this fallacy by incorporating a proper reading of the scope of *Chadha* in the building of formal models. See Elizabeth Martin, "Fast Track and Free Trade: Why Does Congress Delegate?" (Presented at the Annual Meeting of the Midwest Political Science Association, Chicago, April 1992).

61. Joseph A. Davis, "War Declared over Report Language Issue," *Congressional Quarterly Weekly Report* 46 (25 June 1988): 1752.

62. David Rapp, "OMB's Miller Backs away from Report Language Battle," ibid., 46 (9 July 1988): 1928.

63. Miller quoted ibid.

64. Miller's press secretary, Barbara Clay, quoted ibid.

65. See above, note 25.

66. See above, note 25. The disapproval resolutions authorized by the legislative veto mechanism were often tied to expedited procedures. Consequently, such disapproval resolutions were much easier for individual members to initiate and

bring to the floor of the chamber than were actual bills. Irrespective of whether these resolutions were ever enacted, therefore, they were valuable to backbenchers who were unlikely to have much legislative activity attached to their name. The symbolic power of the legislative veto, in other words, was much more valuable to backbenchers than to the congressional leadership.

67. House Committee on the Judiciary, *The Supreme Court Decision in INS v Chadha and Its Implications for Congressional Oversight and Agency Rulemaking: Hearings before the Subcommittee on Administrative Law and Governmental Relations of the Committee on the Judiciary*, 98th Cong., 1st sess., 18 July 1983, 6.

68. Ibid., 125.

69. See above, note 25.

70. OMB Bulletin 83-17, "Proposed Actions Pursuant to Statutes Containing Legislative Veto Provisions," August 10, 1983, 1–3, with appendix.

71. Bernard Weinraub, "Bipartisan Effort: Lawmakers Are to Have Virtual Power of Veto over Program," *New York Times*, 25 March 1989, A1; United Press International, "Bush Counsel Rebuked for Airing a Gripe in the Press; He Rapped New Policy on Contras," *Los Angeles Times*, 27 March 1989, A1; David Hoffman, "Sununu Rebukes Counsel; Chief of Staff Angry at Gray's Challenge to Contra Aid Deal," *Washington Post*, 28 March 1989, A1.

72. Gray's supporters then attacked President Bush for allowing John Sununu, Bush's chief of staff, to silence Gray and uphold Baker's agreement. See Bruce Fein and William Bradford Reynolds, "President Bush's Shameful Surrender," *Legal Times*, 24 April 1989, 16.

73. Louis Fisher, interviewed in Martin Tolchin, "The Legislative Veto, an Accommodation That Goes On and On," *New York Times*, 31 March 1989, A11.

74. For the post-*Chadha* numerical studies that have given rise to these misperceptions, see Louis Fisher, "Judicial Misjudgments about the Lawmaking Process: The Legislative Veto Case," *Public Administration Review* 45 (November 1985): 705–11; Louis Fisher, *Legislative Vetoes Enacted after Chadha*, CRS Report 87-389 (Washington, D.C.: Congressional Research Service, 1987); Fisher, *The Legislative Veto: Invalidated, It Survives*. Those who have made use of these studies to conclude that *Chadha* has been the subject of noncompliance include Michael L. Mezey, *Congress, the President, and Public Policy* (Boulder, Colo.: Westview Press, 1989), 170; John Brigham, *The Cult of the Court* (Philadelphia, Pa.: Temple University Press, 1987), 60–62; James P. Pfiffner, "Divided Government and the Problem of Governance," in *Divided Democracy*, ed. James Thurber (Washington, D.C.: Congressional Quarterly Press, 1991), 56; R. Shep Melnick, *Between the Lines: Interpreting Welfare Rights* (Washington, D.C.: The Brookings Institution, 1994), 30; William T. Gormley, Jr., *Taming the Bureaucracy* (Princeton, N.J.: Princeton University Press, 1989), 209–13; James R. Bowers, *Regulating the Regulators: An Introduction to the Legislative Oversight of Administrative Rulemaking* (New York: Praeger, 1990), 19–23.

75. Peter Strauss explores this problem at length in *Was There a Baby in the Bathwater?*, and in *Legislative Theory and the Rule of Law: Some Comments on Rubin*, 89 Columbia Law Review 427 (April 1989).

76. Ibid., 446 n. 63; Strauss, *Was There a Baby in the Bathwater?*, 814, explains further that "the limited duration of appropriations measures and the practical difficulty the President in any event faces in exercising his veto authority over such measures also suggest a presentment issue far less substantial than that involved when an agency is authorized, for an indefinite term and without presidential participation, to adopt rules as binding as statutes on the public at large, rules which are then made the subject of legislative veto procedures."

77. See above, note 25. For analysis of the origins and development of these informal agreements, known as "reprogramming procedures," see Louis Fisher, *Presidential Spending Power* (Princeton, N.J.: Princeton University Press, 1975), 75–98.

78. *INS v Chadha*, 462 US 919, 968.

79. In his extensive and exhaustive research, Joseph Cooper, "The Legislative Veto in the 1980s," 368, discovered that "roughly three-quarters of the . . . veto provisions enacted into law over the last half-century were enacted in the 1970s."

80. Richard A. Harris, "A Decade of Reform," in *Remaking American Politics,* ed. Richard A. Harris and Sidney Milkis (Boulder, Colo.: Westview Press, 1989), 3.

81. Woodrow Wilson, *Congressional Government: A Study in American Politics* (1885; reprint ed., Gloucester, Mass.: Peter Smith, 1973), 49.

82. House Committee on Rules, *Regulatory Reform and Congressional Review of Agency Rules,* 15 November 1979, 1354 (Allen Schick, Congressional Research Service).

83. For analysis of this phenomenon from Franklin Roosevelt to Bill Clinton, see Sidney M. Milkis, *The President and the Parties: The Transformation of the American Party System since the New Deal* (New York: Oxford University Press, 1993).

84. See Joel D. Aberbach, *Keeping a Watchful Eye: The Politics of Congressional Oversight* (Washington, D.C.: The Brookings Institution, 1990), for analysis of how the increase in congressional oversight activity in the 1970s was tied to increased distrust of executive power in the electorate.

85. House Committee on Rules, *Legislative Veto after Chadha,* 29 February 1984, 458 (Professor Allen Schick, University of Maryland).

86. R. Shep Melnick, *Regulation and the Courts: The Case of the Clean Air Act* (Washington, D.C.: The Brookings Institution, 1983), 5.

87. Aberbach, *Keeping a Watchful Eye,* 44.

88. William West and Joseph Cooper, "The Congressional Veto and Administrative Rulemaking," *Political Science Quarterly* 98 (Summer 1983): 299.

89. House Committee on Rules, *Regulatory Reform and Congressional Review of Agency Rules,* 11 July 1979, 5.

90. House Committee on Rules, *Legislative Veto after Chadha,* 29 February 1984, 463 (Allen Schick).

91. In describing this misconception, Allen Schick noted that "the 1970s demonstrated that legislative vetoes tend to be accompanied by other restrictions; rather than being substitutes for the veto, authorizations and appropriations controls are spawned by the same conditions that spur Congress to subject public agencies to other restrictions." Ibid.

92. *Congressional Record,* 99th Cong., 1st sess., 131, no. 102, daily ed. (26 July 1985): 10155.

93. *Congressional Record,* 99th Cong., 1st sess., 131, no. 101, daily ed. (25 July 1985): 10064.

94. Aberbach, *Keeping a Watchful Eye,* 132, Table 6-1.

95. Ibid., 136.

96. Ibid., 265 n. 23.

97. Craig, *Chadha,* 46.

98. William E. Greider, "Sometimes Congress Does It Right," *Hartford Courant,* 16 September 1980, A15, cited in Craig, *Chadha,* 47 n. 12.

99. See above, note 25.

100. Craig, *Chadha,* 38.

101. President Carter's signing statement noted, however, that "in approving this bill, I want to emphasize my view . . . that section 4 is unconstitutional. Section 4 purports to allow Congress to disapprove agency regulations issued under the [FIFRA] by a concurrent resolution not submitted to the President for his approval. . . . The executive branch will treat section 4 as a 'report and wait' provision and will not consider a congressional expression of disapproval under section 4 to be legally binding." "Federal Insecticide, Fungicide, and Rodenticide Act Extension," signed 16 December 1980: *Public Papers of the Presidents of the United States: Jimmy Carter, 1980–81,* vol. 3 (Washington, D.C.: Government Printing Office, 1982), 2814.

102. Public Law 95-396, 95th Cong., 2d sess., 30 September 1978.

103. *Congressional Record,* 95th Cong., 2d sess., 1978, 124, pt. 22:30212.

104. Ibid.

105. David R. Mayhew, *Congress: The Electoral Connection* (New Haven, Conn.: Yale University Press, 1974), 52–61, defines the term "credit-claimer" as one of the variety of objectives that drive the behavior of members of Congress: claiming credit for doing good is one such objective. For a thorough explanation of the variety of factors that helped the FIFRA statute to pass in 1980, see Christopher J. Bosso, *Pesticides and Politics: The Life Cycle of a Public Issue* (Pittsburgh, Pa.: University of Pittsburgh Press, 1987), 178–206.

106. 7 USC 136(w).

107. See above, note 25.

108. See above, note 25.

109. See above, note 25.

110. In tracking the formal legal impact of *Chadha* on each of the provisions that were operable at the time of the decision in 1983, I found that by the end of 1990, only 25 percent of the provisions had been amended to comply with *Chadha.* The majority, 56 percent of the legally operable provisions, remained unamended. The remaining 19 percent of the provisions expired soon after *Chadha,* or were specifically declared severable in post-*Chadha* litigation. For speculations on why Congress has failed to fix these tainted statutes, see, Elder Witt, "Congress Changes Only Selected Laws In Wake of 1983 Legislative Veto Ruling," *Congressional Quarterly Weekly Report* 44 (6 December 1986): 3028–29. In tracking the legal impact of *Chadha,* I relied on the data base of tainted

provisions compiled by the Office of Legal Counsel of the Justice Department ("Compilation of Currently Effective Statutes That Contain Legislative Veto Provisions," Office of Legal Counsel, Department of Justice, Revised November 4, 1983). The completed data base contains 183 legislative veto provisions that were embedded in 104 different statutes at the time of *Chadha*. I divided each of the 183 provisions into one of three possible outcome categories: the legislative vetoes in question were either "amended," "unamended," or "expired." The "unamended" category contains all those provisions that have remained on the statute books unamended since 1983. The "expired" category contains those provisions that are no longer legally operable because they were in statutes that were terminated, were attached to agency plans or actions that have already been executed, or were declared severable. (When a particular legislative veto provision is found to be "severable" from the statute in which it resides, that statute will continue to operate as if the provision had never been included when the statute was enacted. If it is not severable, the entire statute becomes unconstitutional. The *Chadha* Court held that there should be a presumption in favor of severability unless an examination of the legislative history of the statute in question demonstrated that Congress placed great importance on the legislative veto provision.)

111. See above, note 25.

112. Peter Raven-Hansen, *The Constitutionality of D.C. Statehood,* 60 George Washington Law Review 160, 186 (November 1991). The Fugitive Slave Clause, for example "which has never been repealed, was rendered inoperative," obviously, "by the abolition of slavery." Ibid., 185.

113. Guido Calabresi, *A Common Law for the Age of Statutes* (Cambridge, Mass.: Harvard University Press, 1982).

114. Allan C. Hutchinson and Derek Morgan, *Calabresian Sunset: Statutes in the Shade,* 82 Columbia Law Review 1752, 1763 (December 1982).

115. For comparative analysis, see, Mary Ann Glendon, *The Sources of Law in a Changing Legal Order,* 17 Creighton Law Review 663 (Summer 1984); Martin Harrop, ed., *Power and Policy in Liberal Democracies* (Cambridge: Cambridge University Press, 1992).

116. With the explosion, beginning in the early 1970s, in the number of veto provisions enacted into law, many scholars believed that examining the political significance of the legislative veto mechanism consisted in counting the number of provisions enacted each year, and creating categories with which to distinguish them from each other. In this regard, the most often cited tabulations have been: Joseph Cooper and Patricia Hurley, "The Legislative Veto: A Policy Analysis," *Congress and the Presidency* 10 (Spring 1983): 1–24; Clark F. Norton, *Congressional Review, Deferral and Disapproval of Executive Actions: A Summary and an Inventory of Statutory Authority,* CRS Government Division Report 76-88 (Washington, D.C.: Congressional Research Service, 1976), as supplemented by Norton, *Congressional Acts Authorizing Prior Review, Approval or Disapproval of Proposed Executive Actions, 1976–1977,* CRS Government Division Report 78-117 (Washington, D.C.: Congressional Research Service, 1978); Norton, *Congressional Acts Authorizing Congressional Approval or Disapproval of Proposed Executive Actions, 1978,* CRS Government

Division Report 79-46 (Washington, D.C.: Congressional Research Service, 1979); Norton, *Congressional Veto Legislation in the 96th Congress: Proposals and Enactments,* CRS Government Division Report 82-26 (Washington, D.C.: Congressional Research Service, 1982).

117. In this regard, see James W. Ceaser, *Liberal Democracy and Political Science* (Baltimore, Md.: Johns Hopkins University Press, 1990), 193–94, who discusses how "the Constitution leaves open the precise character and structure of the policymaking process." See also David A. Martin, *The Legislative Veto and the Responsible Exercise of Congressional Power,* 68 Virginia Law Review 253, 293–94 (February 1982), who notes, similarly, that students of American politics are not likely to learn much about the balance of policymaking power from analyzing separation of powers jurisprudence.

CHAPTER FOUR. THE LEGISLATIVE VETO OVER THE FEDERAL TRADE COMMISSION

1. House Committee on the Judiciary, *Congressional Review of Administrative Rulemaking: Hearings before the Subcommittee on Administrative Law and Governmental Relations of the Committee on the Judiciary,* 94th Cong., 1st sess., 21 October 1975, 164–65 (Rep. James J. Blanchard, D-MI).

2. House Committee on Rules, *Regulatory Reform and Congressional Review of Agency Rules: Hearings before the Subcommittee on Rules of the Committee on Rules,* 96th Cong., 1st sess., pt. 3, 15 October 1979, 2.

3. *Congressional Record,* 95th Cong., 2d sess., 1978, 124, pt. 4:5011.

4. Senate Committee on the Judiciary, *Regulatory Reform: Hearings before the Subcommittee on Administrative Practice and Procedure of the Committee on the Judiciary,* 96th Cong., 1st sess., pt. 2, 18 July 1979, 110.

5. Priscilla La Barbera, *Consumers and the Federal Trade Commission: An Empirical Investigation* (East Lansing: Michigan State University, 1977), 19; "Magnuson-Moss" is Public Law 93-637, 93d Cong., 2d sess., 4 January 1975.

6. Bruce K. Mulock, "Legislative Vetoes in Selected Regulatory Agencies," in *Studies on the Legislative Veto,* Report Prepared for the Subcommittee on Rules of the House Committee on Rules, 96th Cong., 2d sess., 1980, Committee Print, 564.

7. Senate Committee on Commerce, Science and Transportation, *Federal Trade Commission Act Amendments of 1989: Report of the Senate Committee on Commerce, Science and Transportation,* 101st Cong., 1st sess., 1989, S.Rept. 101-1249, 2; the explicit authority to prohibit unfair and deceptive practices was added to the original 1914 FTC Act at 15 USC 57a.

8. Robert H. Bork, Statement in *Unfairness: Views on Unfair Acts and Practices in Violation of the Federal Trade Commission Act,* Report Prepared for the Senate Committee on Commerce, Science and Transportation, 96th Cong., 2d sess., 1980, Committee Print, 21.

9. William J. Baer, "At the Turning Point: The Commission in 1978," in *Marketing and Advertising Regulation: The Federal Trade Commission in the 1990s,* ed. Patrick Murphy and William Wilkie (Notre Dame, Ind.: University of Notre Dame Press, 1990), 96.

10. Michael Pertschuk, *Revolt against Regulation: The Rise and Pause of the Consumer Movement* (Berkeley: University of California Press, 1982), 54, 53 n. 16.

11. William J. Baer, *Where to from Here: Reflection on the Recent Saga of the Federal Trade Commission,* 39 Oklahoma Law Review 51, 53 (Spring 1986).

12. Senator Wendell H. Ford (D-KY), quoted in Pertschuk, *Revolt against Regulation,* 54.

13. Jeff Josephs of Chamber of Commerce, quoted in Susan J. Tolchin and Martin Tolchin, *Dismantling America: The Rush to Deregulate* (Boston, Mass.: Houghton Mifflin, 1983), 153.

14. *Congressional Record,* 96th Cong., 2d sess., 1980, 126, pt. 9:11823 (Rep. Bill Frenzel, R-MN).

15. Bernice Rothman Hasin, *Consumers, Commissions, and Congress: Law, Theory, and the Federal Trade Commission, 1968–1985* (New Brunswick, N.J.: Transaction Books, 1987), 108.

16. Congressional Quarterly, Inc., *Regulation: Process and Politics* (Washington, D.C.: Congressional Quarterly, 1982), 51.

17. Barbara Hinkson Craig, *Chadha: The Story of an Epic Constitutional Struggle* (New York: Oxford University Press, 1988), 133.

18. Congressional Quarterly, *Regulation: Process and Politics,* 83.

19. Judy Sarasohn, "Tentative Compromise Reached on Long-Stalled FTC Authorization Bill," *Congressional Quarterly Weekly Report* 38 (26 April 1980): 1148.

20. Caroline E. Mayer, "Court's Veto Ruling Seen as Blow to Business," *Washington Post,* 24 June 1983, D8.

21. *Congressional Record,* 99th Cong., 1st sess., 1985, 131, pt. 15:20450 (Senator Charles Grassley, R-IA).

22. "The FTC as National Nanny," *Washington Post,* 1 March 1978, A22; Federal Trade Commission Transition Team, "Conclusions and Recommendations," *Antitrust and Trade Regulation Report* 999 (29 January 1981): G-1.

23. Michael Pertschuk, *FTC Review (1977–1984): A Report Prepared by a Member of the Federal Trade Commission,* Report Prepared for the Subcommittee on Oversight and Investigations of the House Committee on Energy and Commerce, 98th Cong., 2d sess., 1984, Committee Print, 1.

24. Baer, "At the Turning Point," 105.

25. Mark Silbergeld of Consumers Union, quoted in Caroline E. Mayer, "Dan Oliver: FTC's Head Deregulator Pushes a Broader Agenda," *Washington Post,* 27 April 1987, A9.

26. Richard A. Harris and Sidney M. Milkis, *The Politics of Regulatory Change: A Tale of Two Agencies* (New York: Oxford University Press, 1989), 97; for overview of the Reagan administration strategies that helped reverse FTC activism, see also Robert Katzmann, "Explaining Agency Decision-Making: The Federal Trade Commission and Antitrust Policy in the Reagan Era," in *Handbook of Regulation and Administrative Law,* ed. David H. Rosenbloom and Richard D. Schwartz (New York: Marcel Dekker, 1994), 325–41.

27. Mayer, "Dan Oliver," A9.

28. For discussion of the FTC's inability to exercise its powers because of

budget cuts, see: Senate Committee on Commerce, Science, and Transportation, *FTC Authorization: Hearing before the Subcommittee on the Consumer of the Committee on Commerce, Science and Transportation,* 101st Cong., 1st sess., 7 June 1989, 49; Congressional Quarterly, Inc., *Federal Regulatory Directory* (Washington, D.C.: Congressional Quarterly, 1990), 266, notes that "Reagan's two terms were eight consecutive years of budget and personnel cuts. The FTC work force was cut in half, from 1,800 people when Pertschuk was chairman [during the Carter Administration], to less than 900. . . . Six months into 1981 Reagan trimmed the FTC's budget to $70.8 million. . . . The agency was down to $66.2 million in 1988."

29. Harris and Milkis, *The Politics of Regulatory Change,* 190.

30. Randall L. Calvert, Mark J. Moran, and Barry R. Weingast, "Congressional Influence over Policymaking: The Case of the FTC," in *Congress: Structure and Policy,* ed. Matthew McCubbins and Terry Sullivan (New York: Cambridge University Press, 1987), 504.

31. Ibid., 504–6.

32. The trade regulation rule proposed in 1963 for the Prevention of Unfair or Deceptive Acts or Practices in the Sale of Cigarettes was incorporated in the Cigarette Labeling and Advertising Act of 1965.

33. Barry B. Boyer, "Trade Regulation Rulemaking Procedures of the Federal Trade Commission," in *Recommendations and Reports* (Washington, D.C.: Administrative Conference of the United States, 1979), 42.

34. Timothy J. Muris and Kenneth W. Clarkson, "Introduction," in *The Federal Trade Commission since 1970: Economic Regulation and Bureaucratic Behavior,* ed. Timothy J. Muris and Kenneth W. Clarkson (New York: Cambridge University Press, 1981), 1.

35. See Edward F. Cox, Robert C. Fellmeth, and John E. Schulz, *The Nader Report on the Federal Trade Commission* (New York: Richard W. Baron, 1969), and American Bar Association, *Report of the American Bar Association Commission to Study the Federal Trade Commission* (1969).

36. Timothy J. Muris, "The Federal Trade Commission at Seventy-Five" (unpublished manuscript on file with author, 1991), 72.

37. Boyer, "Trade Regulation Rulemaking Procedures," 42.

38. The Court of Appeals' establishment of rulemaking authority for the FTC came in *National Petroleum Refiners Association v FTC,* 482 F2d 672 (D.C. Cir. 1973).

39. Boyer, "Trade Regulation Rulemaking Procedures," 43.

40. Timothy J. Muris and J. Howard Beales III, *The Limits of Unfairness under the Federal Trade Commission Act* (New York: Association of National Advertisers, 1991), 11.

41. Ibid., 12. In the *S&H* case upholding the FTC's "unfairness" doctrine, the owner of Green Stamps, S&H, was found to have unfairly prevented redeemers of the stamps from offering discounts without S&H approval; *FTC v Sperry & Hutchinson Co.,* 405 US 223 (1972).

42. Roland Brandel and John Sodergren, "FTC and Banking: Power without Limit," *ABA Banking Journal* (June 1982).

43. Boyer, "Trade Regulation Rulemaking Procedures," 43.

44. Charles H. Koch, Jr., and Beth Martin, *FTC Rulemaking through Negotiation*, 61 North Carolina Law Review 275, 289 (January 1983).

45. Ibid.

46. Senate Committee on Commerce, Science and Transportation, *Oversight of the Federal Trade Commission: Hearings before the Subcommittee for Consumers of the Committee on Commerce, Science and Transportation*, 96th Cong., 1st sess., 5 October 1979, 502.

47. Indeed, the "intervenor funding program" established in Magnuson-Moss, a program providing funds to ensure public participation by all interested groups in hybrid rulemaking proceedings, helped make the rulemaking proceedings themselves a source of controversy, since "the list of grants made under the public intervenor program read very much like an honor role of staunch consumer advocates." Harris and Milkis, *The Politics of Regulatory Change*, 174; see also, Barry B. Boyer, *Funding Public Participation in Agency Proceedings: The Federal Trade Commission Experience*, 70 Georgetown Law Review 51 (October 1981).

48. Senate Committee on Commerce, Science and Transportation, *Oversight of the Federal Trade Commission*, 5 October 1979, 508 (Chairman Michael Pertschuk, Federal Trade Commission).

49. Ibid., 19 September 1979, 189 (George Webster and Daniel Piliero, National Fire Protection Association).

50. Koch and Martin, *FTC Rulemaking*, 292.

51. Muris, "The Federal Trade Commission at Seventy-Five," 75.

52. Senate Committee on Commerce, Science and Transportation, *Oversight of the Federal Trade Commission*, 5 October 1979, 507.

53. Boyer, "Trade Regulation Rulemaking Procedures," 57.

54. Muris, "The Federal Trade Commission at Seventy-Five," 82–83.

55. Senate Committee on Commerce, Science and Transportation, *Oversight of the Federal Trade Commission*, 5 October 1979, 523.

56. David Rice, *Consumer Unfairness at the FTC: Misadventures in Law and Economics*, 52 George Washington Law Review 1, 7 (November 1983).

57. Boyer, "Trade Regulation Rulemaking Procedures," 54.

58. Muris and Beales, *The Limits of Unfairness*, 3.

59. Ibid., 14.

60. Senate Committee on Commerce, Science and Transportation, *Oversight of the Federal Trade Commission*, 28 September 1979, 437 (Vincent T. Wasileski, National Association of Broadcasters).

61. Ibid., 18 September 1979, 63 (Senator Wendell Ford).

62. Ibid., 5 October 1979, 509.

63. Federal Trade Commission, *Rulemaking under the Magnuson-Moss Warranty–Federal Trade Commission Act* (Washington, D.C.: Federal Trade Commission, 1979), 31.

64. The irrelevance of constitutional questions, and thus, the irrelevance of *Chadha*, to the functionality of the legislative veto is also evident from examining that part of the veto mechanism that did make something of a practical difference in the regulatory process. In a study devoted specifically to assessing the impact

of the FTC legislative veto, the General Accounting Office concluded that "we identified only one clearly discernible impact on the rulemaking process—FTC added a procedural step to transmit final rules to the Congress." These reporting and waiting requirements associated with the FTC legislative veto remain untouched by the constitutional infirmities struck down by the Supreme Court in *Chadha;* see *Impact of Congressional Review on Federal Trade Commission Decisionmaking and Rulemaking Processes,* GAO/HRD-82-89 (Washington, D.C.: General Accounting Office, 1982), 1.

65. In fact, while some of the proposed versions of Magnuson-Moss included legislative vetoes, the bill that was finally enacted into law in 1975 contained no such provisions because "in general, [Members'] reaction to . . . legislative review of administrative rulemaking has been negative"; see Thomas Nelson, *The Politicization of FTC Rulemaking,* 8 Connecticut Law Review 413, 446 n. 125 (Spring 1976).

66. Senate Committee on Commerce, Science and Transportation, *Oversight of the Federal Trade Commission,* 18 September 1979, 63 (William LaMothe, Kellogg Company).

67. Congressional Quarterly, Inc., *Regulation: Process and Politics,* 87.

68. Baer, "At the Turning Point," 100.

69. Harris and Milkis, *The Politics of Regulatory Change,* 193.

70. Craig, *Chadha,* 217.

71. Senator Robert Packwood (R-OR), quoted in Congressional Quarterly, Inc., *Regulation: Process and Politics,* 87.

72. E. Donald Elliott, "INS v Chadha: The Administrative Constitution, the Constitution and the Legislative Veto," in *The Supreme Court Review 1983,* ed. Philip B. Kurland, Gerhard Casper and Dennis J. Hutchinson (Chicago: University of Chicago Press, 1984), 151.

73. One of the broadest and most stringent of these statutory restrictions reflected congressional frustration with the FTC's "kid-vid" rule, a rulemaking begun in 1978 that was intended to regulate advertising aimed at children. Members enacted a provision in the 1980 Reauthorization that forced the FTC to drop the children's advertising proceeding. The kid-vid rule angered the entire business community in addition to those industry groups that stood to be directly affected by the rule because it justified the regulation of children's advertising simply on the grounds that it was "unfair." Bombarded by constituents' concerns with the potentially unbounded regulation of nondeceptive commercial advertising on the basis of unfairness, members enacted a moratorium on the FTC's use of unfairness in the agency's 1980 Reauthorization. See Tolchin and Tolchin, *Dismantling America,* 164.

74. Elliott, "INS v Chadha," 151.

75. "Funeral Reform Rule Quietly Becomes Law," *Consumer Reports* 48 (July 1983): 325.

76. James W. Singer, "Endangered Species?" *National Journal* 11 (1 December 1979): 2034.

77. Pertschuk, *Revolt against Regulation,* 64.

78. In researching this chapter, the author conducted several interviews, in the

period between January 1991 and May 1992, with current and former FTC staff and FTC commissioners, consumer group lobbyists and lawyers, and lobbyists and lawyers representing trade associations. The names of the interviewees are not mentioned in order to maintain confidentiality.

79. For in-depth analysis of the ways in which Reagan administration appointees dramatically changed the regulatory activities of the FTC, see Harris and Milkis, *The Politics of Regulatory Change*, 140–225.

80. Senate Committee on Commerce, Science and Transportation, *Oversight of the Federal Trade Commission*, 5 October 1979, 505.

81. Ibid., 509.

82. James W. Singer, "Out like a Lamb," *National Journal* 12 (24 May 1980): 867.

83. Federal Trade Commission, *Rulemaking under Magnuson-Moss*, 3.

84. See above, note 78.

85. Senate Committee on Commerce, Science and Transportation, *Oversight of the Federal Trade Commission*, 5 October 1979, 509 (Michael Pertschuk).

86. Ibid.

87. Senate Committee on Commerce, Science and Transportation, Policy Statement on Unfairness, reprinted in *Reauthorization of the FTC: Hearings before the Committee on Commerce, Science and Transportation*, 97th Cong., 2d sess., 18 March 1982, 23.

88. Muris and Beales, *The Limits of Unfairness*, 15–16.

89. Ibid., 25.

90. *Report of the American Bar Association Section of Antitrust Law Special Committee to Study the Role of the Federal Trade Commission*, 58 Antitrust Law Journal 53, 424 (5 April 1989).

91. See above, note 78; for a more thorough explanation of the problems associated with the inability, before Magnuson-Moss, of the FTC to bring suits for consumer redress into federal district court, see Harris and Milkis, *The Politics of Regulatory Change*, 172.

92. See Robert D. Paul, *Federal and State Enforcement Agencies, Current Activities and Priorities: The FTC's Increased Reliance on Section 13(b) in Court Litigation*, 57 Antitrust Law Journal 141, 143–44 (22 March 1988); section 13(b) was added to the original 1914 FTC Act in 1973 at 15 USC 53b.

93. Koch and Martin, *FTC Rulemaking*, 287; the scope of judicial review over FTC rules granted to the courts by Magnuson-Moss was much broader than that generally applied to rulemaking under the APA. Generic APA procedures do not require the court to apply a "substantial evidence standard of review" to the evidence used by agencies in justifying their rulemaking activities.

94. The Vocational Schools Rule was remanded in *Katherine Gibbs School v FTC*, 612 F2d 201 (2d Cir. 1979); the Eyeglass Rule was remanded in *American Optometric Association v FTC*, 626 F2d 896 (2d Cir. 1980).

95. *Katherine Gibbs School v FTC*, 612 F2d 201.

96. *American Optometric Association v FTC*, 626 F2d 896.

97. Ibid.

98. Nelson, *The Politicization of FTC Rulemaking*, 447.

99. See above, note 78.

100. Timothy J. Muris, Director of Consumer Protection, *Food Rule, Phase I*, FTC Memorandum, 1 May 1982, 2.

101. These standards were incorporated into the Statement of Basis and Purpose of the Credit Practices Rule; see Federal Trade Commission, "Trade Regulation; Credit Practices; Final Rule," *Federal Register* 49, no. 42 (1 March 1984): 7740.

102. Ibid., 7742.

103. See above, note 78.

104. See above, note 78.

105. Thomas Stanton, "Comments on the Commission in 1978," in *Marketing and Advertising Regulation*, 112.

106. In addition, the severe budget cuts that the agency began to experience in the early 1980s made it difficult for it to engage in the sort of research that would have produced the rigorous evidence necessary to support rulemakings; see Thomas Maronick, "Current Role of Research at the Federal Trade Commission," in *Marketing and Advertising Regulation*, 348.

107. Larry Reynolds, "The FTC Lion Regains Its Roar," *Management Review* 80 (October 1991): 38.

108. W. John Moore, "Stoking the FTC," *National Journal* 22 (19 May 1990): 1218.

109. Paul M. Barrett and Jeanne Saddler, "Two Regulatory Chiefs Stir Up Business: Under Steiger, FTC Has Ended 'No-Go' Stance," *Wall Street Journal*, 16 May 1991, B1.

110. Existing provisions, however, affected "only a small proportion of the authority Congress has delegated to government agencies"; see Peter Strauss, *Was There a Baby in the Bathwater?* 1983 Duke Law Journal 789, 790 n. 7 (September 1983); see also, Joel D. Aberbach, *Keeping a Watchful Eye: The Politics of Congressional Oversight* (Washington, D.C.: The Brookings Institution, 1990), 134, who notes that "even though the number of statutes with legislative veto provisions had increased dramatically since the veto's introduction in 1932, there were still relatively few statutes even in the late 1970s whose terms allowed a committee to veto, or participate in the veto, of agency regulations."

111. House Committee on Rules, *Congressional Review of Agency Rulemaking: Hearings before the Subcommittee on Rules of the Committee on Rules.* 97th Cong., 1st sess., 19 November 1981, 276 (Rep. Trent Lott, R-MS); see also Richard J. Pierce, Jr., *The Role of Constitutional and Political Theory in Administrative Law* 64 Texas Law Review 469, 483 (November 1985), who notes that "the putatively systematic congressional review that the legislative veto power implies was chimerical; any such review was inevitably sporadic and haphazard."

112. See Craig, *Chadha*, 128, for a description of how the Rules Committee under Chairman Richard Bolling thwarted Rep. Levitas's attempt to obtain support for his generic legislative veto bill.

113. On 21 September 1976, under suspension of the rules, the generic veto bill fell only two votes short of passage (265–135) in the House. See Congres-

sional Quarterly, Inc., *Congressional Quarterly Almanac*, vol. 32 (Washington, D.C.: Congressional Quarterly, 1976), 510. In 1982, the generic legislative veto amendment to the Regulatory Reform Bill was adopted by a 69–25 vote in the Senate. The Regulatory Reform Bill then stalled at the end of the congressional session. See ibid., vol. 38 (Washington, D.C.: Congressional Quarterly, 1982), 524.

114. Alexander Hamilton, James Madison, and John Jay, *The Federalist Papers*, ed. Clinton Rossiter (New York: Mentor, 1961), #14, 100; #27, 174.

CHAPTER FIVE. LEGISLATIVE VETOES IN EDUCATION STATUTES

1. Barbara Hinkson Craig, *The Legislative Veto: Congressional Control of Regulation* (Boulder, Colo.: Westview Press, 1983), 67.

2. K. Forbis Jordan and Wayne F. Riddle, *The Legislative Veto in Federal Education Legislation: Provisions, Their Application, and Alternatives* (Washington, D.C.: Congressional Research Service, 1989), 2. Before the Department of Education was created in 1980, it was the Office of Education within the Department of Health, Education and Welfare (HEW).

3. *Congressional Record*, 99th Cong., 1st sess., 131, no. 165, daily ed. (3 December 1985): 10600 (Rep. William Ford, D-MI).

4. House Committee on Education and Labor, *PL 99-498, Higher Education Amendments of 1986*, 99th Cong., 1st sess., 1985, H.Rept. 99-383.

5. David M. Pritzker and Deborah S. Dalton, *Negotiated Rulemaking Sourcebook* (Washington, D.C.: Administrative Conference of the United States, 1990), 1.

6. *Congressional Record*, 101st Cong., 1st sess., 135, no. 57, daily ed. (9 May 1989): 1719 (Rep. Nick Rahall, D-WV).

7. Chester E. Finn, *Scholars, Dollars, and Bureaucrats* (Washington, D.C.: The Brookings Institution, 1978), 64.

8. Lawrence E. Gladieux and Thomas R. Wolanin, *Congress and the Colleges* (Lexington, Mass.: Lexington Books, 1976), 80.

9. Brian K. Fitzgerald, "Equity and Efficiency: An Analysis of Simplifying the Pell Grant Eligibility Formula" (Ph.D. diss., Graduate School of Education, Harvard University, 1990).

10. 20 USC §1061.

11. Gladieux and Wolanin, *Congress and the Colleges*, 237.

12. *Congressional Record*, 92d Cong., 2d sess., 1972, 118, pt. 5:770.

13. House Committee on Education and Labor, *Elementary and Secondary Education Amendments of 1973: Hearings before the General Subcommittee on Education of the Committee on Education and Labor*, 93d Cong., 1st sess., pt. 3, 26 June 1973, 3000.

14. Ibid., 3005.

15. Ibid., 3011.

16. Ibid.

17. The APA, passed in 1946, established the basic framework of administrative law governing agency action. It imposed due-process procedures on agency

rulemaking, which required agencies to publish a notice of proposed rulemaking in the *Federal Register,* to give interested members of the public a period of time in which to comment on these proposed rules, and to respond to these comments upon publication of final rules; see Administrative Conference of the United States, *A Guide to Agency Rulemaking,* 2d ed., Prepared for the Office of the Chairman by Benjamin W. Mintz and Nancy G. Miller (Washington, D.C.: Administrative Conference of the United States, 1991), 37–89, 169–203.

18. 5 USC §553(a)(2).

19. Cora P. Beebe and John W. Evans, "Clarifying the Federal Role in Education," in *The Federal Role in Education: New Directions for the Eighties,* ed. Robert A. Miller (Washington, D.C.: Institute for Educational Leadership, 1981), 39–48.

20. Harold M. Bruff and Ernest Gellhorn, *Congressional Control of Administrative Regulation: A Study of Legislative Vetoes,* 90 Harvard Law Review 1383 (May 1977).

21. Edward A. Tomlinson, "A Report in Support of Recommendation 78-3: Report on the Experience of Various Agencies with Statutory Time Limits Applicable to Licensing or Clearance Functions and to Rulemaking," *Recommendations and Reports* (Washington, D.C.: Administrative Conference of the United States, 1978), 234.

22. Edith Green, "Federal Funds in Education: When Does Use Become Abuse?" *Educational Forum* 36 (November 1971): 8, 13.

23. This provision is found in §431(b) of the GEPA, known as the Pucinski amendment, 20 USC §1232(a)(1)(b)(1).

24. Tomlinson, "Statutory Time Limits," 234–35.

25. This provision is §431(a) of the GEPA, known as the Green amendment, 20 USC §1232(a); for further discussion, see Theodore Sky, *Rulemaking in the Office of Education,* 26 Administrative Law Review 129, 132 (Spring 1974).

26. Department of Education, "Public Participation in Rule Making," Statement of Policy, *Federal Register* 36, no. 5 (5 February 1971): 2532.

27. Tomlinson, "Statutory Time Limits," 235.

28. These additional requirements are in §431(g) of GEPA, 20 USC §1232(d)(e)(f)(g); for further discussion, see Tomlinson, "Statutory Time Limits," 233.

29. For a description of this aspect of American political culture that begins with a discussion of Tocqueville, see, for example, Robert Goldwin and Robert Licht, eds., *The Spirit of the Constitution: Five Conversations* (Washington, D.C.: American Enterprise Institute,1990), 79–98.

30. For example, the Elementary and Secondary School Act of 1965, the law heralding the federal government's extensive involvement in educational activities, explicitly prohibited OE from exercising "any direction, supervision, or control over the curriculum, program of instruction, administration, or personnel of any educational institution, school, school system, or over the selection of library resources, textbooks, or other printed or published instructional materials by any educational institution or school system." Quoted in Craig, *The Legislative Veto,* 71. Similarly, members worried that reorganizing OE out of HEW into a

Cabinet-level Department of Education would lead the administration to "get off the track" on education policy in ways that "Congress would not be able to control." House Education and Labor Committee, *Oversight Hearing on Congressional Disapproval of Education Regulations: Hearing before the Subcommittee on Elementary, Secondary and Vocational Education of the Committee on Education and Labor,* 96th Cong., 2d sess., 18 September 1980, 63 (Rep. William Ford); consequently, members included a provision in the Department of Education Organization Act stating that the new Department would not "increase the authority of the Federal Government over education or diminish the responsibility for education which is reserved to the States, the local school systems and other instrumentalities of the States." 20 USC §3043; for discussion of this provision, see Senate Committee on Governmental Affairs, *Department of Education Organization Act of 1979,* 96th Cong., 1st sess., 1979, S.Rept. 96-49.

31. The expansion of federal education activities has been characterized by a "proliferation of narrow programs . . . each with its own legislative authorization or separate funding." Joseph Califano, Jr., *Governing America* (New York: Simon and Schuster, 1981), 273. When the Nixon administration tried to cut and consolidate certain education programs, Congress enacted into statute various offices and bureaus within HEW to ensure that such consolidation would not occur. *Congressional Record,* 93d Cong., 2d sess., 1974, 120, pt. 12:15439.

32. Lawrence E. Gladieux and Thomas R. Wolanin, "Federal Politics," in *Public Policy and Private Higher Education,* ed. David W. Breneman and Chester E. Finn, Jr. (Washington, D.C.: The Brookings Institution, 1978), 215.

33. Deborah Rankin, "Educators Assail Student Aid Cuts," *New York Times,* 1 November 1981, A38.

34. In researching this chapter, the author conducted several interviews, in the period between December 1990 and May 1992, with current and former ED and OMB officials, congressional staff from House and Senate Education committees, and lobbyists representing educational associations and institutions. The names of the interviewees are not mentioned in order to maintain confidentiality.

35. Howard Kurtz, "President Yields to Congress, Signs College Student Aid Measure," *Washington Post,* 15 October 1982, A3.

36. Lawrence E. Gladieux, "Student Financial Assistance: Past Commitments, Future Uncertainties," *Academe* (November–December 1986): 10.

37. Rep. Bill Ford, quoted in Califano, *Governing America,* 303.

38. *Congressional Record,* 97th Cong., 1st sess., 1981, 127, pt. 21:27921.

39. Ibid.

40. Ibid., 27922 (Senator Harrison H. Schmitt, R-NM).

41. Ibid.

42. Rep. Simon, quoted in Kurtz, "President Yields to Congress," A3.

43. *Congressional Record,* 97th Cong., 1st sess., 1981, 127, pt. 22:28880–81.

44. Rep. Simon quoted in Kurtz, "President Yields to Congress," A3.

45. Gladieux, "Student Financial Assistance," 10.

46. S.Res. 256, 97th Cong., 1st sess., 10 December 1981.

47. *Congressional Record,* 97th Cong., 1st sess., 1981, 127, pt. 23:30471 (Senator Robert Stafford).

48. Senate Committee on Labor and Human Resources, *The Sallie Mae Technical Amendments Act of 1982*, 97th Cong., 2d sess., 1982, S.Rept. 97-538, 5.

49. See the well-known case studies of the education vetoes by Bruff and Gellhorn, *Congressional Control of Administrative Regulation*, 1369, 1410; Craig, *The Legislative Veto*, 67–97.

50. Tomlinson, "Statutory Time Limits," 236.

51. See, for example, Robert S. Gilmour and Barbara Hinkson Craig, "After the Congressional Veto: Assessing the Alternatives," *Journal of Policy Analysis and Management* 3 (1984): 380.

52. See above, note 34.

53. House Committee on Education and Labor, *Student Loan Consolidation and Technical Amendments Act of 1983*, 98th Cong., 1st sess., 1983, H.Rept. 98-324 (to accompany H.R. 3394).

54. Congressional Research Service, *The Higher Education Amendments of 1986 (PL 99-498): A Summary of Provisions*, CRS Report for Congress 87-187 EPW (Washington, D.C.: Congressional Research Service, 1987), 19.

55. Julie A. Miller, "Cavazos, Bennett, and Bell: First Steps," *Education Week* 8 (21 June 1989): 17.

56. Frances Fitzgerald, "Reagan's Band of True Believers," *New York Times*, 10 May 1987, F36. Bennett was seen as the harbinger of a new vision of public education in the United States. See William Donohue, "Why the Schools Fail: Reclaiming the Moral Dimension in Education," *Heritage Foundation Reports* 172 (23 June 1988).

57. "Tales from the ED," *Education Update* 8 (Spring 1985): 7.

58. Ed Meese quoted in Terrel H. Bell, *The Thirteenth Man: A Reagan Cabinet Memoir* (New York: The Free Press, 1988), 2.

59. "ED Issues Loan-Default Regulations," *Education Week* 8 (21 September 1988): 25.

60. Barbara Vobejda, "Who Should Pay? Federal Aid to College Students Comes under New Scrutiny," *Washington Post*, 9 April 1989, R1.

61. "Statements by Presidents of Historically Black Colleges Following Their Meeting with President-Elect Bush," *Federal News Service*, 11 January 1989; "College District Trustees Oppose Loan Proposal," *Los Angeles Times*, 14 February 1989, B2.

62. Lawrence Eatle quoted in David Baumann, "Student Aid Administrators Bewitched, Bothered and Bewildered over ED Regs," *Education Daily*, 15 April 1988, 6.

63. Tamara Henry, "Rule May Boot Schools from Loan Program," *United Press International*, 13 September 1988.

64. Department of Education, "Student Assistance General Provisions and Guaranteed Student Loan and PLUS Programs," *Federal Register* 53, no. 180 (16 September 1988): 36216.

65. See above, note 34.

66. Lee A. Daniels, "Education: Government Delays Tougher Loan Default Rules," *New York Times*, 28 September 1988, B14.

67. "Stemming Student Loan Defaults," *Los Angeles Times*, 7 April 1989, B6.

68. Department of Education, "Student Assistance General Provisions and Guaranteed Student Loan and PLUS Programs," *Federal Register* 53, no. 194 (6 October 1988): 39317.

69. Julie Kosterlitz, "Losers by Default," *National Journal* 21 (15 April 1989): 921.

70. "Samuel Myers, Executive Director of the National Association for Equal Opportunity in Higher Education, the group that represents the nation's 117 historically black colleges," quoted in Daniels, "Education: Government Delays Tougher Loan Default Rules," 14.

71. Ellen Frishberg, Director of Student Aid, National Association of Independent Colleges and Universities, quoted ibid., 14.

72. *Pell Grant Validation Imposes Some Costs and Does Not Greatly Reduce Award Errors: New Strategies Are Needed,* GAO/PEMD 85-10 (Washington, D.C.: General Accounting Office, 1985), 3.

73. 1981 General Accounting Office report cited ibid., 9.

74. Ibid., vi.

75. House Committee on Education and Labor, *Oversight on Current Status and Administration of Federal Student Assistance Programs: Hearing before the Subcommittee on Postsecondary Education of the Committee on Education and Labor,* 97th Cong., 2d sess., 4 February 1982, 303 (A. Dallas Martin, Jr., National Association of Student Financial Aid Administrators).

76. See Susan Boren, *The Pell Grant Program: Background and Issues,* CRS Report for Congress 89-411 EPW (Washington, D.C.: Congressional Research Service, 1989), 5.

77. See above, note 34.

78. Department of Education, "Student Assistance General Provisions and Pell Grant Program; Verification of Application Information," *Federal Register* 51, no. 50 (14 March 1986): 8946.

79. Ibid.

80. See above, note 34.

81. House Conference Report, *Higher Education Amendments of 1986,* 99th Cong., 2d sess., 1986, H.Rept. 99-861. President Reagan recognized this provision regarding "the accuracy of basic aid application information" as a direct attack on one of Bennett's policies and objected to it because it "improperly limits the discretion of the Secretary of Education to manage programs effectively." But Reagan did not veto the bill containing the provision. "Higher Education Amendments of 1986," *Weekly Compilation of Presidential Documents,* Administration of Ronald Reagan (17 October 1986), 1411.

82. David Tatel, former head of ED's Office of Civil Rights, quoted in Kenneth J. Cooper, "Scholarship Policy Called Not Binding; Revision Is 'Personal Opinion' That Lacks Force, Ex-Official Asserts," *Washington Post,* 20 December 1990, A20.

83. House Committee on Government Operations, *Department of Education's Race-Specific Scholarship Policy: Hearings before the Human Resources and Intergovernmental Relations Subcommittee of the Committee on Government Operations,* 102d Cong., 1st sess., 20 March 1991, 33.

84. Ibid., 21 March 1991, 82 (Richard Komer, Deputy Assistant Secretary for Policy).

85. Ibid., 81.

86. ED published a Notice of Proposed Policy Guidance on the issue in the *Federal Register* after having published a request for public comment. See Department of Education, "Non Discrimination in Federally Assisted Programs; Title VI of the Civil Rights Act of 1964," *Federal Register* 56, no. 237 (10 December 1991): 64548; Department of Education, "Student Financial Aid Programs in Which Race, Color or National Origin Is a Factor," *Federal Register* 56, no. 104 (May 30, 1991): 24383.

87. "Keeping College Doors Open," *Christian Science Monitor,* 19 December 1991, 20.

88. Ibid.

89. Secretary Alexander's attempt to withhold the recognition of the Middle States Association of Colleges and Schools as an accrediting agency, because of its use of a diversity standard, represents a similar case. Outraged at the secretary's attempt to bypass reporting requirements in this manner, members forced him to reconsider his proposed policy change. Middle States had its recognition reinstated. See House Committee on Government Operations, *Civil Rights, Diversity, and Accreditation: Hearing before the Human Resources and Intergovernmental Relations Subcommittee of the Committee on Government Operations,* 102d Cong., 1st sess., 26 June 1991; and Karen DeWitt, "Accrediting Agency Wins Renewed Federal Approval," *New York Times,* 15 April 1992, B11.

90. See above, note 34.

91. See above, note 34.

92. See above, note 34.

93. See above, note 34.

94. See above, note 34.

95. Senate Committee on Labor and Human Resources, *The Sallie Mae Technical Amendments Act of 1982,* 6.

96. See above, note 34.

97. See statement of Rep. Nick Rahall regarding the loss of the legislative veto, and ensuing general discussion about the reg negs in the Hawkins-Stafford Elementary and Secondary Education Improvement Amendments of 1988 in *Congressional Record,* 101st Cong., 1st sess., 135, no. 57, daily ed. (9 May 1989): 1719. For general background on reg-neg procedures, see "Recommendations of the Administrative Conference, Procedures for Negotiating Proposed Regulations," *Federal Register* 47, no. 136 (15 July 1982): 30708.

98. Those who participated in the 1988 Elementary and Secondary Education Act reg neg "were glad to have been part of the negotiation and said they felt a distinct sense of ownership of the regulations as a result of their participation." They expressed particular appreciation for the opportunity to build relationships with ED and with other practitioners involved in implementing regulations. See Elizabeth R. Reisner, Joanne Bogart, and Janie E. Funkhouser, *Evaluation of the New Rulemaking Requirements Implemented in the Development of the 1989*

Chapter 1 Regulations, U.S. Department of Education, Office of Planning, Budget and Evaluation (March 1989), 38–39. Those who participated in an earlier reg neg conducted by EPA involving asbestos removal in schools heralded the procedure as one that allowed the education community "a much bigger arena to voice our concerns." Julie Miller, "ED to Try 'Negotiated Rulemaking' Process," *Education Week* 7 (17 February 1988): 15. Soon after the 1988 reg neg was conducted, Congress enacted another mandatory reg neg into the Vocational Education Act of 1989.

99. *Congressional Record,* 101st Cong., 1st sess., 135, no. 57, daily ed. (9 May 1989): 1763 (Rep. Harry Bartlett, R-TX).

100. See above, note 34.

101. Department of Education, "State Vocational and Applied Technology Education Programs and National Discretionary Programs of Vocational Education," *Federal Register* 56, no. 198 (11 October 1991): 51448.

102. See above, note 34.

103. See above, note 34.

104. See above, note 34.

105. In defining "representative" functions, Roger Davidson and Walter Oleszek draw on the *Federalist Papers,* the writings of Edmund Burke, and a survey of historical studies and contemporary political analysis: "Studies indicate that public officials and citizens view the twin functions of elected assemblies— lawmaking and representing—as separate, definable tasks." And in observing American constitutional practice, Davidson and Oleszek affirm that "Congress has been responsible for the dual functions of *lawmaker* and *representative assembly.*" Roger H. Davidson and Walter J. Oleszek, *Congress and Its Members,* 4th ed. (Washington, D.C.: Congressional Quarterly, 1994), 4–6.

Chapter Six. Legislative Vetoes over Presidential Authority to Extend Most-Favored-Nation Status

1. Prior to the post–Cold War activities meant to aid economic development in Eastern Europe, the Trade Act of 1974 represented the exclusive manner in which a nonmarket economy (NME) country could be granted most-favored-nation treatment and become eligible for other trade benefits from the United States. Jeanne J. Grimmett, *Trade Agreements with Nonmarket Countries: Chadha, the Trade Act, and Constitutional Authority over Foreign Commerce,* CRS Report for Congress 90-197A (Washington, D.C.: Congressional Research Service, 1990), 1–2; for analysis of Nixon administration objectives regarding the Trade Act of 1974, see Walter F. Mondale, "Beyond Detente: Toward International Economic Security," *Foreign Affairs* 53 (October 1974): 15.

2. For discussion of the congressional opponents to the Nixon administration's forging of the Trade Act legislation, see Paula Stern, *The Water's Edge: Domestic Politics and the Making of American Foreign Policy* (Westport, Conn.: Greenwood Press, 1979), 59.

3. Kenneth Klein, *The Trade Act of 1974: Soviet-American Commercial Relations and the Future,* 5 Georgia Journal of International and Comparative Law 505, 528 (1975).

4. These statutory restrictions would prevent the president from concluding any commercial agreements, or extending MFN treatment, or U.S. credit or investment guarantees to a nonmarket economy country that "1) [denied] its citizens the right or opportunity to emigrate; 2) [imposed] more than a nominal tax on emigration or on the visas or other documents required for emigration, . . . or 3) [imposed] more than a nominal tax, levy, fine, fee, or other charge on any citizen as a consequence of the desire of such citizen to emigrate to the country of his choice." These restrictions were codified at 19 USC §2432(a).

5. Vladimir N. Pregelj, *Jackson-Vanik Amendment and Granting Most-Favored-Nation Treatment and Access to U.S. Financial Programs to the Soviet Union*, CRS Report for Congress 89-686E (Washington, D.C.: Congressional Research Service, 1989), 2–3.

6. Senate Committee on Finance, *The Trade Reform Act of 1973: Hearings on H.R. 10710 Before the Committee on Finance*, 93d Cong., 2d sess., pt. 2, 7 March 1974, 457 (Henry A. Kissinger, Secretary of State).

7. 19 USC §2432(c)(1).

8. Grimmett, *Trade Agreements with Nonmarket Countries*, 17.

9. 19 USC §2432(d)(5).

10. 19 USC §2435(a),(c).

11. Senate Committee on Finance, *Trade Reform Act of 1974*, 93d Cong., 2d sess., 1974, S.Rept. 93-1298, 3.

12. Jeanne J. Grimmett, *The Effect of INS v Chadha on Section 402 (Jackson-Vanik Amendment) of the Trade Act of 1974*, CRS Report for Congress 90-49A (Washington, D.C.: Congressional Research Service, 1990), 12. Arguing in favor of the veto provisions, Senator Howard Cannon (D-NV) noted, as did many other members involved in the House and Senate debates regarding the enactment of Jackson-Vanik in 1974, that "the provisions under the amendment we are debating will give the Congress ample authority to review the results of the waiver, and the Congress will definitely use this authority." *Congressional Record*, 93d Cong., 2d sess., 1974, 120, pt. 30:39801.

13. Paul Lansing and Eric C. Rose, *The Granting and Suspension of Most-Favored-Nation Status for Nonmarket Economy States: Policy and Consequences*, 25 Harvard International Law Journal 329, 346–47 (Spring 1984).

14. See, for example, statements of Robert Herzstein, Esq., Arnold & Porter, and of Laszlo Hamos, Chairman of the Committee for Human Rights in Romania, in Senate Committee on Finance, *Continuation of the President's Authority to Waive the Trade Act Freedom of Emigration Provisions: Hearing before the Subcommittee on International Trade of the Committee on Finance*, 98th Cong., 1st sess., 29 July 1983, 65, 196–205.

15. Ibid., 48 (Michael Matheson, Deputy Legal Adviser, U.S. Department of State).

16. Ibid., 49.

17. Through annual presidential waivers of Jackson-Vanik restrictions, China received MFN status every year since Congress approved the U.S.-China Bilateral Trade Agreement in 1980.

18. This was the first disapproval resolution pursuant to the legislative veto provisions in Jackson-Vanik ever passed by a chamber of Congress.

19. Michael S. McMahon, *The Jackson-Vanik Amendment to the Trade Act of 1974: An Assessment after Five Years,* 18 Columbia Journal of Transnational Law 525, 531 (1980); see also Martha Liebler Gibson, *Weapons of Influence: The Legislative Veto, American Foreign Policy, and the Irony of Reform* (Boulder, Colo.: Westview Press, 1992), 83–106.

20. Michael W. Beasley, Thomas F. Johnson, and Judith A. Mather, *An Interim Analysis of the Effects of the Jackson-Vanik Amendment on Trade and Human Rights: The Romanian Example,* 8 Law & Policy in International Business 193, 196 (1976).

21. Ibid., 197.

22. "Text of Kissinger Statement on Accord Cancellation," *New York Times,* 15 January 1975, A4.

23. "Under the Nixon Administration," Stevenson and Frye point out, "the number of émigrés leaped from barely 200 in 1968 to almost 35,000 in 1973. After passage of the Jackson-Vanik Amendment, the exodus fell sharply to 13,000 in 1975." Adlai E. Stevenson and Alton Frye, "Trading with the Communists," *Foreign Affairs* 68 (Spring 1989): 54–57.

24. William Korey, "Jackson-Vanik and Its Myths," *Midstream* 35 (August–September 1989): 10.

25. Cynthia Dachowitz, *The Soviet Denial of the Right to Emigrate: An Economic Response,* 11 Brooklyn Journal of International Law 325, 351 n. 185 (Spring 1985).

26. 12 USC §635e(b). The Stevenson amendment ceilings on financial credits "would almost shut the door on" any benefits the Soviets would otherwise have received in return for complying with Jackson-Vanik freedom of emigration requirements. William Korey, "The Jackson-Vanik Amendment in Perspective," *Soviet Jewish Affairs* 18 (Spring 1988): 45.

27. Ibid., 39.

28. Ibid.

29. Korey, "Jackson-Vanik and Its Myths," 10.

30. Korey, "Jackson-Vanik in Perspective," 40.

31. Stern, *The Water's Edge,* 186.

32. The legislative veto provisions in the Stevenson amendment had no effect on Congress's control of the $300 million credit ceiling. The veto provision allowed Congress to approve, through a concurrent resolution procedure, the president's requests to raise the credit ceilings. The president could not, in other words, raise the credit ceilings without express congressional approval. The Supreme Court's invalidation of the procedure simply required Congress to comply with the presentment clause. This had no policymaking impact on the statutory requirement for congressional approval.

33. 19 USC §2432(a)(1).

34. 19 USC §2432(a).

35. Senate Committee on Finance, *President's Authority to Waive Freedom of Emigration Provisions,* 325-26 (Frank Koszorus, Jr., International Human Rights Law Group).

36. House Committee on Ways and Means, *Extension of Most-Favored-Nation*

Treatment to Romania: Hearing before the Subcommittee on Trade of the Committee on Ways and Means, 94th Cong., 2d sess., 14 September 1976, 1.

37. H.Res. 1547, in *Congressional Record*, 94th Cong., 2d sess., 1976, 122, pt. 24:30557.

38. House Committee on Foreign Affairs, *United States-Romanian Relations and Most-Favored-Nation (MFN) Status for Romania: Hearing before the Subcommittee on Europe and the Middle East of the Committee on Foreign Affairs*, 100th Cong., 1st sess., 30 July 1987, 26.

39. W. Gary Vause, *Perestroika and Market Socialism: The Effects of Communism's Slow Thaw on East-West Economic Relations*, 9 Northwestern Journal of International Law & Business 213, 269 n. 237 (Fall 1988); House Committee on Foreign Affairs, *United States-Romanian Relations and Most-Favored-Nation Status*, 24 (Rozanne L. Ridgway, Assistant Secretary of State).

40. 19 USC §2432(c).

41. "Joint Statement of Principles Following Discussions with President Ceauşescu of Romania," signed in Washington, 1973: *Public Papers of the Presidents of the United States: Gerald Ford, 1975*, vol. 1 (Washington, D.C.: Government Printing Office, 1977), 576.

42. House Committee on Ways and Means, *Extension of Nondiscriminatory Treatment to Products of Romania*, 94th Cong., 1st sess., 1975, H.Rept. 94-359, 3.

43. Senate Committee on Finance, *Bilateral Commercial Agreement between the United States and the Socialist Republic of Romania*, 94th Cong., 1st sess., 1975, S.Rept. 94-281, 3.

44. House Committee on Ways and Means, *United States-Romanian Trade Agreement: Hearings on H.Con.Res. 252 before the Subcommittee on Trade of the Committee on Ways and Means*, 94th Cong., 1st sess., 7 May 1975, 38.

45. Senate Committee on Finance, *Bilateral Commercial Agreement*, 3; House Committee on Ways and Means, *Extension of Nondiscriminatory Treatment*, 7.

46. Vladimir N. Pregelj, *Most-Favored-Nation Policy toward Communist Countries*, CRS Issue Brief IB74139 (Washington, D.C.: Congressional Research Service, 1987), 13.

47. Senate Committee on Finance, *President's Authority to Waive Freedom of Emigration Provisions*, 7 (Senator Henry Jackson).

48. All Senate and four House resolutions died in committee: S.Res. 171, 98th Cong., 1st sess. (1983) (Romania); S.Res. 428, 97th Cong., 2d sess. (1982) (Romania); S.Res. 555, 94th Cong., 2d sess. (1976) (Romania); H.Res. 234, 99th Cong., 1st sess. (1985) (Romania); H.Res. 570, 97th Cong., 2d sess. (1982) (China); H.Res. 775, 96th Cong., 2d sess. (1980) (Romania); H.Res. 1547, 94th Cong., 2d sess. (1976) (Romania). One House resolution died when a motion to discharge from the House Ways and Means Committee was tabled: H.Res. 475, 99th Cong., 2d sess. (1986) (Romania). All other House resolutions were reported adversely and, with one exception, were indefinitely postponed: H.Res. 258, 98th Cong., 1st sess. (1983) (China); H.Res. 257, 98th Cong., 1st sess. (1983) (Hungary); H.Res. 256, 98th Cong., 1st sess. (1983) (Romania); H.Res. 521, 97th Cong., 2d sess. (1982) (Romania); H.Res. 653, 95th Cong., 1st sess. (1977) (Romania).

49. H.Res. 317, 96th Cong., 1st sess. (1979) was defeated by a vote of 126 to 271. Only the disapproval resolution directed at disapproving MFN for China in 1990, H.J.Res. 647, 101st Cong., 2d sess. (1990), succeeded in being passed by one house. This special case will be discussed below.

50. *Congressional Record,* 100th Cong., 1st sess., 1987, 133, pt. 13:17739.

51. Ibid., 17745.

52. Bureau of National Affairs, "State Department Notes Emigration Gains, Says Other Factors Figure in Trade Waiver," *International Trade Reporter* 6 (15 February 1989): 205.

53. Bucharest Agerpres, "Statement on the Economic Relations of the Socialist Republic of Romania with the United States of America," *Bucharest Agerpres* (Embassy of the Socialist Republic of Romania) press release on file with author, February 27, 1988, 2.

54. In researching this chapter, the author conducted several interviews, in the period between December 1990 and May 1992, with current and former officials of the United States Trade Representative, the Department of State, congressional staff, and lobbyists with experience of international trade policymaking under Jackson-Vanik. The names of the interviewees are not mentioned in order to maintain confidentiality.

55. "The inclusion of human rights improvements as a condition for preferential trade status is an important development. Congress, by its vote on suspension of Romanian MFN, has placed human rights discussion as a priority in bilateral relations and we hope that this development will continue to motivate decisions concerning increased trade and relations." Reps. Tony Hall (D-OH), Frank R. Wolf (R-VA), and Chris Smith (R-NJ), *End of MFN for Romania,* "Dear Colleague" letter on file with author, 29 April 1988, 1.

56. "[Rep. Donald] Pease [D-OH] introduced HR 4939 to set new human rights conditions for China to meet before the President could waive Jackson-Vanik for another year in 1991." John R. Cranford, "House Passes Bills to Punish China for Tiananmen Action," *Congressional Quarterly Weekly Report* 48 (20 October 1990): 3490.

57. House Committee on Foreign Affairs, *Most-Favored-Nation Status for the People's Republic of China: Hearings before the Subcommittees on Human Rights and International Organizations, Asian and Pacific Affairs, and on International Economic Policy and Trade of the Committee on Foreign Affairs,* 101st Cong., 2d sess., 16 May 1990, 4 (Rep. Christopher Smith, R-NJ).

58. Senator John Danforth (R-MO) argued against the incorporation of additional human rights conditions into Jackson-Vanik by claiming that "we took the position that Jackson-Vanik meant that emigration was the sole condition for most-favored-nation status, and we should not extend that further." *Congressional Record,* 102d Cong., 1st sess., 137, no. 112, daily ed. (22 July 1991): 10529.

59. These "technical amendments" to the statute, which were enacted as part of the "Mini–trade bill" of 1990, were

intended to remove the possibility [that] procedures in Title IV might be unconstitutional, without changing the underlying scheme of the law. . . . The Jackson-Vanik Amendment, section 402 of the Trade Act of 1974, prohibits MFN for NME countries unless they meet certain standards relating to freedom of emigration, but the President is authorized to waive these conditions under certain circumstances. However, if his waiver is disapproved by either House of Congress within 60 days after he makes the waiver, then his waiver authority with respect to the country concerned is invalid. . . . The defect is cured . . . by a provision of the bill amending the law to make the resolution of disapproval a joint resolution. Since the resolution of disapproval would, unlike the existing law, be subject to Presidential veto and the Congress overriding the veto, the Committee bill allows 45 days in addition to the time allowed under current law for this process to be completed. (Senate Committee on Finance, *An Act to Make Miscellaneous and Technical Changes to Various Trade Laws,* 101st Cong., 2d sess., 1990, S.Rept. 101-252, 51–52)

60. House Committee on Foreign Affairs, *Most-Favored-Nation Status for the People's Republic of China,* 265.

61. John R. Cranford, "Trade and Foreign Policy: The Ties That Bind," *Congressional Quarterly Weekly Report* 48 (9 June 1990): 1777.

62. These bills conditioning China's MFN status on improvements in human rights conditions received so much support so quickly that commentators expected them to be enacted: they seemed "likely to result in new conditions for the extension of MFN status to China." Lucille A. Barale, "U.S. MFN Renewal for China: The Jackson-Vanik Amendment," *East Asian Executive Reports* 12 (June 1990): 9.

63. Rep. Sam Gibbons (D-FL), quoted in Cranford, "Trade and Foreign Policy," 1777.

64. See above, note 54.

65. *Congressional Record,* 100th Cong., 1st sess., 1987, 133, pt. 8:10688.

66. Ibid., 10691 (Rep. Bill Frenzel, R-MN).

67. John R. Cranford, "Committee Links China Status to Progress on Rights," *Congressional Quarterly Weekly Report* 48 (29 September 1990): 3102.

68. Ronald D. Elving, "Bill Links China's MFN Status to Human Rights Progress," *Congressional Quarterly Weekly Report* 48 (14 July 1990): 2200.

69. *Congressional Record,* 102d Cong., 1st sess., 137, no. 105, daily ed. (10 July 1991): 5317 (Rep. Donald Pease).

70. Cranford, "Committee Links China Status," 3102. As with critics of the bills conditioning MFN status for Romania in the mid–1980s, critics of the bills conditioning China's MFN status tried to dissuade their colleagues from voting for them by claiming that they would be just as draconian as enacting disapproval resolutions: Senator John Danforth claimed that the result of a conditionality bill "would be to terminate most-favored-nation status. . . . Maybe that is what we want to do. . . . But let us not delude ourselves that there is such a thing as a middle ground, that there is such a thing as conditional most-favored-nation status." *Congressional Record,* 102d Cong., 1st sess., 137, no. 112, daily ed. (22 July 1991): 10528.

71. *Congressional Record,* 99th Cong., 2d sess., 1986, 132, pt. 13:17960.

72. See above, note 54. Knowing full well that Rep. Richard Schulze's disap-

proval resolution would be vetoed if it received enough congressional support to reach the president, members who supported it believed that threatening to "cancel MFN immediately [would] bring stiff pressure on China to change its human rights policies." Cranford, "Committee Links China Status," 3102.

73. See above, note 54.

74. *Congressional Record,* 102d Cong., 1st sess., 137, no. 105, daily ed. (10 July 1991): 5317.

75. See above, note 54.

76. House Committee on Foreign Affairs, *Most-Favored-Nation Status for the People's Republic of China,* 232 (Richard Solomon, Assistant Secretary of State).

77. Ibid., 18.

78. Ibid., 22.

79. See above, note 54.

80. Rep. Solarz warned that "we give MFN to a whole series of repressive regimes with respect to which we express our concerns about their violation of human rights in other ways." House Committee on Foreign Affairs, *Most-Favored-Nation Status for the People's Republic of China,* 123.

81. *Congressional Record,* 102d Cong., 1st sess., 137, no. 113, daily ed. (23 July 1991): 10669.

82. For extended discussion of Jackson's role in blocking the Carter administration's proposal, see Robert M. Dow, Jr., "Senator Henry M. Jackson and U.S.-Soviet Detente" (D.Phil. thesis, Oxford University, 1996), 286–91.

83. Ronald D. Elving, "Emigration Holdup Snags Soviet Pact," *Congressional Quarterly Weekly Report* 48 (26 May 1990): 1640.

84. See above, note 54.

85. See above, note 54.

86. Cranford, "Trade and Foreign Policy," 1774.

87. Members have made sure to take advantage of these fast-track procedures even though they have preferred to express their objections through conditions bills independent of the Jackson-Vanik statute rather than through the proscribed disapproval resolutions. Since conditions bills are technically independent of the statute, they are not covered, as are disapproval resolutions, by Jackson-Vanik expedited procedures. Members have therefore always introduced conditions bills coincidentally with the annual cycle of the waiver review. By piggybacking conditions bills on disapproval resolutions in this way, members have ensured that the bills reach the floor for a vote of the full chamber.

88. "Despite the president's constant and consistent claim that he would veto any conditions bill, no matter how mild," explained one of the USTR staff members who worked on China's MFN extension in 1991, "there was great momentum during the 102d Congress to pass such a bill." See above, note 54.

89. *Congressional Record,* 102d Cong., 1st sess., 137, no. 112, daily ed. (22 July 1991): 10519.

90. H.J.Res. 647 (1990) threatened to terminate MFN for China soon after the Tiananmen Square massacre.

91. Cranford, "House Passes Bills to Punish China," 3490.

92. 19 USC §2435(c).

93. U.S.-Romanian Trade Agreement approved under the congressional review

procedure of Jackson-Vanik in August 1975; U.S.-Hungarian Trade Agreement approved July 1978; U.S.-China Trade Agreement approved February 1980. See Pregelj, *Most-Favored-Nation Policy toward Communist Countries*, 10, 12, 15.

94. Senate Committee on Finance, *An Act to Make Miscellaneous and Technical Changes to Various Trade Laws*, 52.

95. The concurrent resolutions in the Jackson-Vanik bilateral trade agreement approval procedure were tainted by *Chadha* because concurrent resolutions fulfill the bicameralism requirement of the Constitution, but not presentment.

96. See above, note 54.

97. See above, note 54.

98. See above, note 54.

99. This amendment essentially preserved the status quo; requiring the president to approve Congress's approval of a presidential proposal is not much different from simply requiring Congress to do the approving. Amending a concurrent resolution of approval into a joint resolution of approval did not, in other words, make much practical difference.

100. Senate Committee on Finance, *An Act to Make Miscellaneous and Technical Changes to Various Trade Laws*, 52.

101. Ibid., 52. A joint resolution requires compliance with bicameralism and presentment.

102. See House of Representatives, *Determination of Hungary's Laws and Policies with the Trade Act*, 101st Cong., 1st sess., 26 October 1989, H.Doc. 101-104, 1.

103. See Public Law 102-182, 102d Cong., 1st sess., 4 December 1991.

104. See above, note 54.

105. See above, note 54.

106. This includes the Clinton administration.

107. U.S. Department of State Fact Sheet, "Most-Favored-Nation (MFN) Trade Status for China," May 1990, 1.

108. Cited in *Congressional Record*, 102d Cong., 1st sess., 137, no. 112, daily ed. (22 July 1991): 10519.

109. See above, note 54.

110. See above, note 54.

111. *Congressional Record*, 102d Cong., 1st sess., 137, no. 113, daily ed. (23 July 1991): 10668.

112. Keith Bradsher, "Bush Said to Order China Import-Barrier Inquiry," *New York Times*, 10 October 1991, A18.

113. Thomas L. Friedman, "Baker Asks China to Free Prisoners," *New York Times*, 16 November 1991, A3.

114. Adam Clymer, "China Rebuff Seems Unlikely to Hurt Trade Status," *New York Times*, 19 November 1991, A8; see also, Thomas L. Friedman, "Baker's China Trip Fails to Produce Pledge on Rights," *New York Times*, 18 November 1991, A1.

115. Though members kept introducing disapproval resolutions annually after *Chadha*, Jackson-Vanik did not, technically, "contain a constitutionally acceptable process for congressional review of a presidential recommendation of a waiver" until 1990, when the unconstitutional one-house vetoes and concurrent

resolutions were amended to constitutional forms. Barale, "U.S. MFN Renewal," 12.

116. Before *Chadha,* none of the bills introduced in Congress threatening to alter the respective powers of the executive and legislative branch over MFN extensions addressed the scope of Jackson-Vanik linkage: within two weeks of the enactment of the Trade Act in 1974, a bill was introduced re-establishing only the provisions of the original, waiverless Jackson-Vanik amendment; see H.R. 1265, 94th Cong., 1st sess. (1975). Bills were also introduced to relax the conditions for issuing the Jackson-Vanik waiver to a communist country. These extended the term of the president's waiver authority from one to five years, for example, and eliminated the assurances requirement; see S. 339, 96th Cong., 1st sess. (1979), and H.R. 1835, 96th Cong., 1st sess. (1979).

117. See above, note 54.

CHAPTER SEVEN. CONCLUSION

1. Linda Greenhouse, "Warren E. Burger Is Dead at 87; Was Chief Justice for 17 Years," *New York Times,* June 26, 1995, A1, B6.

2. House Committee on Rules, *Congressional Review of Agency Rulemaking: Hearings before the Subcommittee on Rules of the Committee on Rules,* 97th Cong., 1st sess., 28 October 1981, 228 (Rep. George Danielson, D-CA).

3. Ibid.

4. Ibid., 7 October 1981, 201.

5. See, for example, ibid., 28 October 1981, 217–18 (Rep. George Danielson): "Do we really need a veto? . . . We are fighting [a] strawman. . . . I respectfully submit that if a rule comes along which we find so offensive that it stirs our blood . . . . , if we simply communicate that fact to the agency, they would pay quite a bit of attention to it."

6. Woodrow Wilson, *Congressional Government: A Study in American Politics* (1885; reprint ed., Gloucester, Mass.: Peter Smith, 1973), 203.

7. In other words, Wilson's political science is "above all opposed to anything smacking of formalism." Harvey C. Mansfield, Jr., *America's Constitutional Soul* (Baltimore, Md.: Johns Hopkins University Press, 1991), 6.

8. Eldon J. Eisenach, *The Lost Promise of Progressivism* (Lawrence: University Press of Kansas, 1994), 73, 106; for a definition of "Progressivism," and the problems associated with trying to define it, see Daniel T. Rogers, "In Search of Progressivism," *Reviews in American History* 10 (December 1982): 113–32.

9. Bert A. Rockman and R. Kent Weaver, eds., *Do Institutions Matter? Government Capabilities in the United States and Abroad* (Washington, D.C.: The Brookings Institution, 1993).

10. Alexander Hamilton, James Madison, and John Jay, *The Federalist Papers,* ed. Clinton Rossiter (New York: Mentor, 1961), #34, 207.

11. Wilson, *Congressional Government,* 54 (emphasis added).

12. *The Federalist Papers,* #55, 344.

ACKNOWLEDGMENTS

In researching and writing this book, I have been blessed with guidance from wonderful teachers, thoughtful criticisms from generous colleagues, and unwavering support from friends and family. My curiosity about the dynamics of American political development was sparked by Stephen Skowronek in a memorable undergraduate seminar at Yale University. Then, in the government department at Harvard University, Paul Peterson directed my study of politics and political institutions with focus, energy, and enthusiasm. Under his shrewd mentoring, I developed the ideas, acquired the practical knowledge, and honed the interpretations that make up this book.

Also in the government department, Harvey Mansfield's writings and lectures brought to life for me the history of political theory. His gracious responses to my incorrigible questioning enriched my understanding of the principles of American constitutionalism. The late Judith Shklar, with characteristic sternness and warmth, made sure that my graduate studies in political science remained part of, and continued to be informed by, a broad education in the liberal arts. And Kenneth Shepsle, by guiding my reading, enabled me to benefit from Positive Political Theory scholarship on American political institutions.

At key stages of this project, Mark Peterson and R. Shep Melnick gave me valuable advice on research design and execution. From Alan Morrison's seminar at Harvard Law School I received a comprehensive introduction to separation of powers jurisprudence. And I am indebted to my fellow graduate students Robert Lieberman, Daniel Stid, and Patrick Wolf for important contributions to the original framework of this study and for continuing suggestions, over many years, on how to improve it.

Most of the research for this book was conducted while I was a research fellow in the governmental studies program of the Brookings Institution in 1990–91, and a guest scholar for various periods during 1991–93, and then again in the fall of 1995. I am delighted to acknowledge the intellectual debts I incurred at Brookings to Keith Banting, William Frenzel, Steve Hess, Robert Katzmann, Keith Krehbiel, Thomas Mann, Gary McKissick, Pietro Nivola, Eric Patashnik, R. Kent Weaver, and Julian Zelizer, and especially to my fellow research fellows, Bruce Bimber, Tom E. Sugrue, and Philippe Klinkner. I also owe thanks to the over one hundred government officials and industry representatives who, through repeated interview sessions under the condition of anonymity, shared with me their insights about the workings of the American policymaking process.

The political science department at the University of Massachusetts at Amherst proved a wonderful place to complete most of the writing for this book. In particular, Peter Haas, John Hird, Jerry Mileur, M. J. Peterson, and Jeffrey Sedgwick gave generously of their time and thought in commenting on numerous drafts of this study.

I was very fortunate that the entire manuscript was subjected to the learned and thorough commentary of Daniel Farber, Sidney Milkis, Jeremy Rabkin, and Jeffrey Tulis. Derek Bok and Louis Fisher also read parts of the manuscript and made extremely helpful observations. Early in the process, Theda Skocpol, a series editor of the Princeton Studies in American Politics series, gave me wise counsel. Malcolm DeBevoise, former law and political science editor at Princeton University Press, his successor Malcolm Litchfield, and their assistant Heidi Sheehan, facilitated the completion of this project through their unfailing support. Beth Gianfagna and Gavin Lewis provided masterful production management and copyediting.

Selected portions of this book have been adapted from journal articles I wrote, with permission of the publishers: *Institutional Reforms That Don't Matter: Chadha and the Legislative Vetoes in Jackson-Vanik,* 29 Harvard Journal on Legislation 455 (Summer 1992); "Improving the Policymaking Process By Protecting the Separation of Powers: *Chadha* and the Legislative Vetoes in Education Statutes," *Polity* 26 (Summer 1994): 677–98; "The Legislative Veto and the Limits of Public Choice Analysis," *Political Science Quarterly* 109 (Winter 1994–95): 873–94.

For financial support, I thank the government department at Harvard University, the Brookings Institution, the Mellon Foundation, the department of political science at the University of Massachusetts, and the Massachusetts Institute for Social and Economic Research. For administrative support, I am grateful to Anthony Oettinger, chairman of the Program on Information Resources Policy at Harvard University, and John White, former director of the Center for Business and

ACKNOWLEDGMENTS

Government at the Kennedy School of Government. They made it possible for me to finish this book while beginning the research for a new study. Stephen Coelen and Noel Yu of the Massachusetts Institute for Social and Economic Research enabled me to keep abreast and take advantage of emerging computer technologies intended to facilitate research and writing. And for speedy, high-quality research assistance, I have Lawrence Becker, Jennifer Stump, and Jeanne Sheehan Zaino to thank.

In many and creative ways, and with an ever-present generosity of spirit, Sheri Berman, Jill Blickstein, Katie Dunn Tenpas, Lauren Osborne, and Gideon Rose assisted me in putting this project to rest. And I am grateful to Peter Berkowitz for his patient criticism, steady encouragement, and wise judgments in helping me clarify the arguments of this book.

NAME INDEX

NAME INDEX

NAME INDEX

NAME INDEX

GENERAL INDEX

GENERAL INDEX

About the Author

JESSICA KORN is Assistant Professor of Political Science at the University of Massachusetts at Amherst and a 1995–1996 American Political Science Association Congressional Fellow.